Daniel Berrigan, Jesuit priest, author, and vice chairman of the American Fellowship of Reconciliation, is currently involved, as always, with matters of life and death. In addition to his participation in resistance to the arms race, he serves, on a part-time basis, in a hospital devoted to the care of persons dying of cancer. Among his recent books published by The Seabury Press are *A Book of Parables, Uncommon Prayer: A Book of Psalms,* and *Beside the Sea of Glass: The Song of the Lamb.*

Robert F. McGovern, whose woodcuts appear in *The Discipline of the Mountain*, is a a painter, sculptor and print-maker, who teaches at the Philadelphia College of Art and lives in Narbeth, Pennsylvania. In addition to illustrating several books, his work has also appeared in *New Covenant Magazine* and the *Catholic Worker.* He is also known for his church architectural work and has had 11 one-man exhibitions.

The Discipline
of the Mountain

Also by Daniel Berrigan

PROSE
The Bride: Essays in the Church
The Bow in the Clouds
Consequences; Truth And
Love, Love at the End
They Call Us Dead Men
X *Night Flight to Hanoi*
No Bars to Manhood
The Dark Night of Resistance
X *America Is Hard to Find*
The Geography of Faith (with Robert Coles)
Absurd Convictions, Modest Hopes (with Lee Lockwood)
Jesus Christ
Lights on in the House of the Dead
The Raft Is Not the Shore (with Nhat Hanh)
A Book of Parables
Uncommon Prayer: A Book of Psalms
Beside the Sea of Glass: The Song of the Lamb
The Words Our Savior Taught Us

POETRY
Time Without Number
No One Walks Waters
Encounters
The World for Wedding Ring
False Gods, Real Men
Trial Poems (with Tom Lewis)
Prison Poems
Selected and New Poems

DRAMA
X *Trial of the Catonsville Nine*

Daniel Berrigan

THE
DISCIPLINE
OF THE
MOUNTAIN

*Dante's Purgatorio
in a Nuclear World*

illustrations by
Robert McGovern

A Crossroad Book • *The Seabury Press* • New York

In Loving Memory
Honor Berrigan
1921–1979

1979 • The Seabury Press • 815 Second Avenue • New York, N.Y. 10017
Copyright © 1979 by The Seabury Press Inc.
All rights reserved. No part of this book may be reproduced,
stored in a retrieval system, or transmitted, in any form or by
any means, electronic, mechanical, photocopying, recording, or
otherwise, without the written permission of The Seabury Press.

Printed in the United States of America

Library of Congress Cataloging in Publication Data

Berrigan, Daniel.
The discipline of the mountain.
"A Crossroad Book."
I. Dante Alighieri, 1265–1321. Divina commedia.
Purgatorio. II. Title
PS3503.E734D5   851'.1   79–9379
ISBN 0-8164-0296-5

Contents

Here are reproved and restored the souls once wasteful of life. A dialogue ensues; the differences between brute and human creation set forth.

In which a hideous vision assaults the pilgrim. The chimera is overcome by intervention of Dante. The Mountain of Purgation quakes with deliverance, exaltation.

Of the pope who grasped at honors more than service, and the effects thereof. Strange variations, by night and day, in conduct of Penitents of Avarice. The plight of the secret Christian revealed.

The sin of gluttony exposed. The penitents, their expiation; thirst, abstinence. In which also the Discipline of the Mountain is explained in some detail. A mysterious tree, then a second, come into view.

A question vexes the pilgrim. A gracious soul enlarges on matters of guilt, healing. Purgation of lust by fire. The pilgrim enters the flames, issues forth unharmed. Dante abruptly bids the pilgrim farewell.

The pageant of glory unfolds. Beatrice appears; matters long hidden are peremptorily raised by the lady. The pilgrim confesses; she in turn prophesies.

In which the cruel ascent of the Mount of Purgation is at length consummated. *Finis coronat Opus*: a vision of Christ and the church.

Introduction

It was consequent on long reflection (and an equally long series of actions) that I began my study of Dante. One lives today, trying to imagine our plight, a plight shadowed, first of all, by nuclear event as prophecy. What is God saying to us, what would he have us do, as a seemingly irreversible course leads humanity, like a blindfolded beast, toward the abattoir? Might there be ways of coping, ways which might properly be named spiritual, that is to say, surpassing whatever the politics of Left or Right might offer?

Ways of imagining our plight. Few such ways are at hand. Only the brute facts are at hand; and they serve, by and large, not to energize, offer joy, relief, perspective, community voice, but to spin one further into a vortex of despair or anomie.

Possession of the facts is, in sum, as futile as ignorance. Those who are ignorant of the facts shut their doors against the polluting winds, and go on. They cling to one or two private myths—about religion, about America—clutch them like household gods, incant them against the noisy unknown, hold on. They put out the flag, they go to church.

Those in possession of the facts are hardly better off, nor should their conduct be praised. I am thinking mainly of those who once struggled against the Vietnam war. Facts of·life today notwithstanding, we see little of them any more. They have taken the facts into the wilderness. Some academics among them actually trumpet the dreadful facts (arms race, neutron bombs, consequent world poverty) as evidence that America must continue "on course." It is all to the good, it is virtuous, it is above all necessary. For, as every sane skull knows, we have "an Enemy."

If these false prophets happen to be religious, they are in possession of a powerful additional weapon, an ideology of note. Not only as citizens must we be enlisted in a bone chilling cold war; it is as believers. For if citizens have an enemy, Christians have an antiChrist. Onward next generation of holocaust weaponry. And what of the next generation of humans? We are not told.

Long experience led me to the conclusion: Politics, Left or Right, offers no alternative. As commonly understood and practiced, it is a sham, a waste. Right, Left, they cannot rise; but they do converge.

To imagine our plight. Not to fantasize about it, a flight from the realities before us. Not to suppress it, a plight too heavy to be borne. I do not think it too heavy to be borne; together with friends (most of whom bore the burden more gracefully, knowledgeably, conscientiously than I) it could be borne. Indeed, unless we are all to give up before the ironbound inevitable, must it not be borne?

A faithful vision, an alternative, a tradition. A truthful image of God, of ourselves, of history. Clumsily put, these were what I was groping for. I noted, in contrast, a plague of "how-to" handbooks for Christians; they seemed to me mildly insane, a low-grade narcotic. And they sold, as the expression goes, like mad.

I was fed up with "how to." I thought the truth of the matter was closer to "what if?" What if the world, in the Christian eye, appeared not as a limbo for the inert, nor a hell for the self-damned?

What if Dante were right? What if this place and time were a laborious ascent to God, to beatitude? A preliminary world, a world in the making?

What if, in a bad time, our conduct, our imagination, our friendships, our falling back and pressing on, our prayer, our agonies and depression of spirit, the vision that keeps us going, keeps us from greater despair—what if these counted, had meaning, were taken into account by Another?

And what if, at the same time, a gracious gift were at work in us, hinting when all seems lost, that all is not lost (though nearly all may be lost)? Hints of possibility, fresh starts, confessions of guilt, delays, reflection, deeper scrutiny of conscience, pain and resolution of pain. What if?

I began to study Dante in a bilingual edition. Started by setting down notes, phrases, then whole sections. Not a translation by any means, the *terza rima* in English seemed beyond my scope; and in any case a dead form. Another difficulty arose; the events and personages Dante worked into his poem only served to embed large sections of the *Purgatorio* in the thirteenth century.

I had to think about his method, concrete as well as philosophical, political, passionately personal. How might those themes, moods, discourses, encounters be adapted, come alive today?

Dante's Caesarean church repelled me. *Arbiter mundi*, aping the great ones, mourning lost ground, miffed at kings and princes for not playing games of power according to her rules. As though indeed kings and princes and colonels and shahs and juntas could be prodded into secular pacifism (whatever that might be), or rule this world from the Mount of the Sermon. The church on an equal footing with high-handed secular powers? We have different agonies today. And a far less grandiose understanding of who we are vis-à-vis this world; humiliated, "pruned," as John's gospel has it, far less assured, more improvisational, obscurely searching. Christians, I thought, will know what I am groping for.

The *Purgatorio* is unique within the *Commedia*. The *Paradiso* and the *Inferno* are on the church's traditional ground. Dante voyaged to hell and heaven as a spectator, exalted, horrified in turn—

but a bystander. Moreover, in both, the ethics, the arrangements of justice, reward, punishment are conformed to the orthodoxy of pulpit and Bible. Horrors of sense, deprivation of God's presence on the one hand; on the other, glory, beatific vision. He is verifying a tradition already well attested to—a tradition which he imbibed through a porous culture of art and word.

But the *Purgatorio* is his own. This biblical man, this sensitive and finely tuned mind, this traditionalist, is also nervy and undaunted, an innovator. Did he find traditional purgatory, those subterranean regions of fire spoken of in sermons and tracts, not simpatico with his temperament, his sense of Christ? In any case, he struck out on his own. He imagined an immensely lofty mountain of pilgrimage, delay, penance, a kind of Crogh Patrick of the spirit. And then he climbed it; or rather, he beckoned the dead along with him, appointed Virgil his guide, and proceeded to follow—where in fact he could only have led.

Less dogma surrounds purgatory, a region lying somewhat to the side of the eye; neither ecstasy nor damnation. Rather, a kind of passionate waiting game goes on there, played out by souls who on earth have been wasteful, neglectful of responsibility, grace. This was a capital point with Dante; purgatory was firmly anchored in this world, in time.

He imagined souls sentenced to purgation in accord with their time serving or disserving on earth. At the foot of the mountain, souls hunker about; the time of their denial of entrance is equivalent, in one way or another, to the time they have let go, wasted, badly used on earth.

The point is a striking one, crucial to the art, as well as to Dante's view of human nature. If indeed there exists a continuity of conscience and self-understanding between this world and another, then, among other benefits, human dignity is honored. Nothing is wasted, including judgment on the high quality or shabbiness of moral action. Nothing is overlooked, nothing falls in a void. The absurd, the rock of Sisyphus, is itself rendered absurd. All this struck me like a bolt. It is the reason why, at a comparatively late time of my life, I began to study the *Purgatorio*. There was that tantalizing question: Did Dante conceive purgatory as a world apart from our own, attached to ours only by the frail cable of suspended questioning? Or was purgatory joined to our world, as a mountain to a plain, as (in the moral order) consequence is joined to conduct?

Here and now, purgatory. And Dante within it, attesting to its reality, identifying its faces, toting up its crimes and reprisals, its hard-won joys, gratitude, moral victories. He sees with bodily eyes its angels and invisible spirits and forms, including our own forms, souls. A world only slightly out of focus with what our eyes, our ears hear, our eyes touch. As indeed the essential quality and forms, the truth of things, must always be out of focus, out of style, out of "relevance," in comparison with the lies and semblances which this world hucksters as truth.

This, as far as I can understand, is the only real strangeness of the *Purgatorio*. Not the strangeness of another physical world, of Mars contrasted with Earth. Nor the strangeness of mere allegory (though allegory is certainly one of his methods).

Something different, disturbing, because shot through with the familiar and the unfamiliar all at once. Somewhat as though Jesus had kept a diary of his forty days in the Judean desert. Demons, hallucinations perhaps, presentiments of the future; the liberated, the damned, the near blessed, pressing on him their malignancy, blessings. A record of many strange things seen, attested to, truth and untruth; telling much, hinting at more.

Or I think of mountains of pilgrimage, journeys of intercession, the seven-story mountain of Merton. If a pilgrim, fasting, were to keep a record of a nightlong vigil on such a mountain, we might well have another hint as to Dante's method. The cold, fasting, the sleepless vigil—all work on the brain. One sees things, understands things not granted to mortals at sea level. There are encounters through the long night with other penitents, seekers—strangers become friends. Recognition scenes. Outstretched arms across a chasm of years and years. On such nights we are told that the dead walk abroad, no strangers to the living. Gross occupations, lifelong distractions, the appetitive soul weighing down the body, the body dragging its appetites through the world of sense and slavery—do not these prevent access to a world of truth? Come, let us enter the discipline of the mountain.

Dante was a son of the church. This is the great honor I can pay him. By it I mean something quite simple and crucial. He draws clean lines. He knows the Gospel and its other face, betrayal; in himself first of all, then in others, including those in high places. He knows the complexity of life in the world, how it sinks some under, bears others along, always uneasily. And he is not bewitched by complexity, ambiguity; he does not make a vocation out of head scratching. No, there are sin and error and foolishness, rancor, ill will, lust. These are not fabrications to keep people in line, names unattached to realities. They are sin. He says so.

And there is redemption; hope beats on, never gives up. As long as time lasts, there is possibility of blessedness, against all hope, against the main chance. It is a word Dante spoke first of all, to himself. And for this I thank him, that he did not exempt himself from the fate of humans, but set himself firmly on the mountain where all must work out the salvation they have betrayed or scorned. He is there, ascending, wondering, doubting, confessing—and judged. One to one he goes, with his friend and teacher, ascending through clutter and darkness to lucid essentials, discovering what a human being might be, a human life, a life worth living. Renewing the symbols that sustain, foster, lend stature, beget clairvoyance and courage. He makes life new, he walks in spite of all, sure footed.

It is called a tradition; it is the stark opposite of a dead religion. Dante knew it; he could not merely inherit such riches, nest in them, live off them. (In this respect, he reminds me of the canny investor spoke of by Christ.) What then to do? He was a poet and a public man; he would move the tradition along, a spider thread from his being, telling, testing as he went.

He called to his side one who had done something like this, long before, Virgil. Because, it seems, he wanted an "opposite number," in Gandhi's phrase. In the manner of the truly great who, seek a loving adversary, a friend who will tell the truth, especially the unpleasant truth. Someone unsubdued by leveler Death, someone creaturely. One who had made a like voyage, a world wandered, creator of heroes, and more. In Dante's eyes, Virgil was mentor, moral teacher, guide, a kind of secular saint. Exactly, as things turn out, and with necessary nuances, what Dante became to me.

Dante's was a time, one remembers, that trumpeted its greatness on every wind. It was a time of dazzling innovative art, of the new vernacular poetry. The center was holding; synthesis was the intellectual mode; Christendom turned a confident face on the empire, the world beyond. It could afford to be generous. Were not its glories evident, intact?

And along with all this (as it seems, must be true in every imperial age)—violence. Dante lived with it, was immersed in it. As leader of one warring faction, he inevitably became its victim.

As it turned out, exile was his salvation. (As I learned too, both in 1965 and again in 1970, when I read with bitter relish and a nod of recognition: "How bitter to taste the salt of another's bread, and climb another's stair.")

Still, it seems to me that without the suffering, dependence, wanderings and, above all, the solitude and study of those nineteen years of banishment, we would have had no *Commedia*.

The imperial stereotype. Florence: Not just a city, more like a state; wars, its own coinage, trade, flag, ambassadors. Above all, wars. And when foreign wars were lacking, internal fighting, bloody conflicts of interests. Does it evoke a tic, recognition? The leading candidates for slaughter in Dante's lifetime (he belonged to one of them) were the Blacks and the Whites.

Florence was a minute image of Rome. Arrangements were not working well; above all, they worked ill for Dante. Still, he thought for a long time that Rome had worked well. He was not granted to see, in other words, that no imperium in history has "worked well"—if by the phrase we mean something approaching the evangelical commonweal; implying access by all to justice, to the goods and services of the realm, public officials who serve instead of battening, no prisons or sanctioned state murder, and so on.

Dante was blind to these grievous shortcomings in his social order. Indeed, in the *Purgatorio* he enshrined the social arrangements of the empire in his esthetic and political vision. He still thought, even in his great poetry, that the church-imperium arrangement was of divine origin, that the destitute condition of the times was due to reparable malice, simony, ego. But that the arrangement was literally "in the nature of things," that it was a divine plan. Alas, we know otherwise.

One is tempted to dwell on this seductive mirage, the imperial plan as mirror of the divine plan. The Bible dissolves it in two ways. First by pointing out the self-destroying forces that lie within every empire, and inevitably bring it down. By concluding, inferentially, that the empire has but one destiny: self-destruction.

Secondly, by insisting that the empire, any empire, is simply an idol. The sum of its energies, structures, gears, fuels, wealth, trade, ideologies, pledges of allegiance, loyalty oaths, armies, cargoes, navies, air forces, marines, secular covenants, and so on—all these lie under the empire of the spiritual powers, they are a hieratic order of death. Christians, who purportedly owe other allegiances, must walk a wary way round these enticing sirens, threats, vows, promises, utopias. Christians are called, not to enlist in the state, but to suffer at its hands.

And to narrow the case to Dante's own, Florence could be expected to "work" no better than Rome, whose unworkability was celebrated in the Book of Revelation. Revelation linked Rome with defunct Babylon, itself linked hand in glove with still older histories of collapse, death. The biblical word is unmistakably clear; but who, in any empire, reads the Bible?

Without pushing things, Florence, and the pseudo-tradition it stands with and for, reminds me of our own times and country. Of Washington, Moscow, Peking. But one should speak of one's own turf—of oneself. Americans, too, have the dizzy, inflated sense of themselves which the demons confer. In our case, too, nagging doubts engender rigid certainties. Material grandeur, media puffing; tawdry though the paradise be, inaccessible to most, still it puts off such questions as Dante raised (but only at a distance, in solitude and suffering). Questions of wisdom, of happiness. Are we happy? We forget to ask ourselves, but faces tell us.

At high level or low, in the empire technique is all. It is the demonic soul of imperial conduct, activity in the world. It is also killingly competitive; in nuclear matters it demands isolation, policing, secrecy. In its service citizens become slaves of Mars.

Dante summoned Virgil, an act of piety, ancestral honor. He did so also, I think, in order to set limits, to declare the boundaries of reality. Virgil indeed guides Dante through that "less cruel sea," up the Mount of Purgation. But, just short of blessedness, Beatrice appears on the scene. And Virgil simply vanishes. He is not suddenly transfigured or canonized. But here, now, nature ends; grace invites. Through Virgil, Dante traces the outer reaches of the possible.

Dante is not dogmatic in all this. He is something infinitely better, rarer. He is a truth teller.

He creates the mountain, a godlike act, and its more or less guilty inhabitants, more or less burdened and blinded, skinny from fasting, immobilized by their past, icy or burning with fever. Each in process of being reborn, restored, healed.

They know him, they converse with him, he is indeed one of them. One of them! Recognition scenes are the poignant heart of his conquest of death, a conquest drawn entirely from the Gospel promise. I will not dwell on what this means, that our faith stands in defiance of death; what it might mean to others who dwell in our death-shot century.

In Dante's century, as now, death was an acceptable method— of dealing with enemies, of furthering one's interests, of making a place in the world.

The question is, who will say yes? If we are politically bound, hand and foot, if madmen armed to the teeth pretend to speak for us, to kill in our name—if all this is true (and it is sadly and literally true), then the question is by no means annulled; it grows all the more urgent. Who will say yes? The question rises from the throats of prisoners and the tortured and defamed of earth, innocent, victimized, at the mercy of the powers. Who will say yes?

Dante says yes. Not cheaply, not comfortingly, not with one eye on orthodoxy and another fixated on the pain of the world. But with a whole heart, with all his might, with "two eyes making one in sight," with a courage that dares take into account hell, despair; our fragile, ludicrous, tragic fate. The accuracy of his master image is tested in a most painful and humiliating way; that is to say, it includes him, draws him in, judges him.

My sins. My guilt. My responsibility. My unfinished, indeed self-wounded humanity. My betrayals. My waste of time and grace. And above all and beyond all and beckoning me forward, my hope, which is not mine at all, but gift, grace, calling.

Dante walks there, converses, suffers, pays up. It is all quite simple, direct, concrete, episodic, worldly, here and now. In several episodes things are pushed hard. He meets souls expiating sins he himself has been guilty of. Such moments are cruelly truthful; he is stopped in his tracks. At the terrace of lust he walks the flames, as he tells us, in such agony that "immersion in boiling glass would have spelled relief."

Confessional poetry indeed. Beatrice calls out; the only time in all the *Commedia* when his name is spoken. The lips of transfigured love recognize the poet. But Beatrice is no mere comforter; indeed there are few moments in literature more disconcerting than this one. Beatrice stands before him, a Valkyrie of God, an accuser! In a culture that makes of judgment a dirty word, whose rules decree that no one may be called to accounts—in such a world, the lover who judges, the judge who is lover, these are indeed anomalous. What are we to make of this unfashionable, scriptural, metaphysical sternness?

The episode invites a long reflective look, implying as it does responsibility, forgiveness, power of love victorious over death.

Dante weeps. As a prelude to forgiveness. His tears fall on good soil. Indeed, we are in "another world."

Dante walks among the dead. He arouses wonderment and awe (to us, it is the dead who arouse wonderment and awe) because his flesh and blood are solid, he casts a shadow. He mingles with those souls, commiserates with their suffering, though he knows their suffering is exacted in justice, and so do they. But he mourns, he is one of them. Like a short-term prisoner, he promises to bring back messages to the living. He wants to be found acceptable, to be useful in their helplessness.

In every encounter, he is apt to normalize, solidify, verify emotion; the cords of Adam even in that place, bind, hold firm.

Access to the unseen? It is possible, Dante says, but not to pander to comfort, hot or cold; there are to be no ambiguous mutterings in half-darkened rooms. Transactions with the dead, heartbreaking attempts at embraces, all come to pass in broad daylight, in bracing, sun-drenched air. Indeed the geography, height, location of the mountain are matters of great concern. Its measure is taken again and again, at every time of day. Sun and stars are in place. Dante's imagination is exact as a master astronomer's. We must understand that his mountain *exists*—on our planet, in a system of planets, verified, at just such distance from Jerusalem or Rome.

It is one thing to imagine, it is a quite different thing to mystify. In the *Purgatorio* there is no relief from the human condition. That condition, burdened, humiliated, guilty, at once implacable and devious in evil resolve, is everywhere insisted on. Friends say it and enemies: Behold us, we died as we lived. But hear us out, for a mercy greater than malice has intervened.

They show their wounds, they hold up their ravaged faces, beg his intercession and that of the church on earth.

No mystification here. No explaining away of guilt. Dante pays the souls (ourselves) the sublime honor of responsibility; there is lengthy discoursing on this theme. The dead are sinners, they are ourselves. That is to say, they (we) are wounded in our humanity, clouded in understanding, willful and self-deceived as to the truth, resourceful at self-deception. Longing for salvation, shying away from it. Fleeing from that "ragged figure, flitting from tree to tree at the back of the mind."

There was a dualism to be overcome. To those on earth, the dualism of heaven and hell is irrefragable, beyond reversing.

They—we. They condemned or transfigured, we on earth, neither buried in torment nor wheeling in bliss. Indeed the dualism here is so strictly in accord with the nature of things, that to dissolve it offends against reality. To accept heaven or hell as images of this world, is to nullify our world.

We see such extremes in our culture: beatitude, despair, flight from reality, flight from responsibility, from the unbearable pain of life. But there is no flight in the *Purgatorio*. Every step is uphill, every step costs and counts. Dante wearies, cries out, grows disheartened, he suffers pain of spirit, remorse. His mind recoils, all but unhinged with grief at the plight of those he has called friends on earth. He cannot understand, must seek counsel. Emotion is drawn out, purified. It is not a dream of reality he invokes. It is reality imagined and undergone.

This is what drew me to the *Purgatorio*, a sense that Dante had dissolved the we—they, this world—other-world impasse. He came upon (created, better) a world whose difference from this world is the difference between the appearance of things and the truth of things. And he said to Virgil (to ourselves): Walk with me. He said to Virgil: Instruct me. And all the while, this cunning spirit is instructing us. To make sense, to make art, Dante had to climb, to risk.

One danger lies particularly close in matters of the spirit: The we-they, the doctrine of several worlds, can easily degenerate into an I-it impasse. The believer, that is to say, can refuse to enter the mountain. He can plant himself in this world, hold the guidebook, refuse the journey. In so doing, he loses communion with the body of believers, whose vitality, symbols, world understanding, ethic, imaginative sources beckon us on the march.

The great refusal cancels the journey. Then the faith becomes a mere list of dogmas, leaving the will to fend for itself, the emotions frozen. The "I" no longer delights in the "we"; the faith is now a mere "it."

Much ink has been spilled, most of it in vain, around the question of Dante's system of purgatory. Does he offer more than a caricature of human acts, placing lust, anger and so on, like square pegs in square holes, in a landscape labeled "Seven Deadly Sins"? Can God judge us more lucidly than we judge ourselves? Has not the area of guilt and accountability become a mine field, littered with the corpses of pre-Freudian error? There is, in fact, little that could be called arbitrary about his system. His choice of *seven* (sins, terraces) is an old game of numbers, a symbol of limits; it suggests here (as it often suggests in scripture) a rounding off of life, a longing, reaching for perfection. The seven terraces coalesce in a structure; there, one may observe, enter, grasp the drama of salvation. Parallel structures come to mind: the unities of Greek drama or the plan of an Elizabethan theater. Like the Mount of Purgation, these offer a setting, a geography, a cosmos susceptible to heroic struggle.

Finally the climb levels off, the air clears. Flames of purgation surround those who sing as they endure; their deliverance to the heavenly meadows adjoining their place of torment nears.

On that height we, too, can breath deep, purified, anticipating. On the threshold of blessedness, we look back; the long climb is over at last. Shortly we will stand in a place just short of paradise. There the grandeur, justice, compassion of the Creator is at long last vindicated. Angels have chastened and beckoned us; Beatrice has judged, purged, acquitted. We are at length what we are called to be.

1·Invocation

The Beginning

It was that day the Christian heart
(stalled between hope and hell)
missed beat—
that day Christ confounded
the powers of death and hell
His siege perilous
hardly begun   was over

This day   this day
my journey began   out of this world
(deeper into this world)
        I would penetrate
            the lying semblances   the feverish fits and starts
            the chimeras   stalking appetites
(the ghastly smiles   switch blades of my street)
        that dark muddled sack
            the modern world

a journey
a task
        —to learn from the dead –
        A mountain   exigent   dangerous
    honeycombed   like a Hopi village
with weird   eyeless   all seeing tribes

building like starfish   new limbs   organs   souls
dormant   ignored   unused on earth
        feverishly misused on earth

Having come to a middle ground
            a measure of dry wisdom
        toted up resources
                    Had come through
    the whiff of hell   the taste of death
detention   courts   public spectacle
        Time to move on.   Time
        moved on.   Time said
        Move On.

Dante   first pilgrim of that mountain
            prime mover of imagination
        eloquent   unitive
He leaps from the page like a
        winged foot on the uphill climb

Him I choose for guide   mentor;   *Come with me*
    brother   near saint   near hero
        Irony   disclaimer
        lend savor to the soul
                I pray; Do not take me
    too seriously   Do not push religion
        in thin air   do not confuse
    the real world   with the errant
        appetitive psyche   Confusion in such matters
        works great mischief

    I summoned him   intoning
            Per correr migliori a que alza a le vele
omai la navicella del mio ingegno
la lascia dietro a se mar si crudele

He stood before me   modern spirit
soul of wit and fire   benign   quicksilver
but stern too   a face the dead put on
soul's final form

That beginning!
in a meadow
where the mountain started upward
like a turbulent thought
clouding the brow of God
In that meditative meadow
on a spring morning
the Almighty
took counsel with himself—
then
an encompassing gesture—
So be it! death no dominion!
I will raise him up!

In that meadow
my Dante   light and truth
bent   spread his hands
in pure dew
anointed me
sealing   signing my true condition—
pilgrim of the absolute

We climbed laboriously that rock face
sun at our backs   sun ahead   a weird sun dance
between huff and puff I spoke to my friend
    Will the journey always be arduous?
    Only at first   Time will come
when the sheer levels off   Finally the passage so eases
    you'd think yourself drifting   summering downstream.

> Still we dragged ourselves upward upward
> a ledge stood under our feet
> There we sank   speechless   exhausted

The ascent begins on Easter morning. Indeed, what better time? From the start, the journey of a soul is put in clear focus. It is not "going it alone." It is one with the journey of Christ, through death and rebirth.

Thus, at a single stroke, Dante (and we) place ourselves at the center of things. We would be where Christ is, go where he has gone. Our deepest sense of ourselves, of the human road, of an existence reasonably free of vagaries and moral inertia, takes us in his direction. Indeed we confess that, apart from his direction, our so-called path is no more than a labyrinth.

His; the ascent of mount Calvary. And prior to that, the ascent of the Mount of Beatitudes; there the terms, demands, pace, tenor, spirit of the Kingdom were first proclaimed. And finally on the Mount of Ascent Jesus takes the world and history and the living to his great heart, mounting above, converging within. Indeed Dante (and we) have both map and mapmaker for the journey at hand.

The invoking of Dante is of course imagined. It is imagined secondhand; no such things took place in the original *Commedia* (in which of course, the invoking of Virgil is imagined).

I can only say in justification, what Virgil was to Dante, Dante became for me.

The best the neophyte can say, in company with the skilled and courageous is: I am willing to try.

Perhaps with such a spirit as Dante's, noting the guideposts he has planted, studious after those stern, singular, earthy, exacting, ethically exciting images—with these, with him to point them out, I may make my way without doing or suffering notable damage. May even offer a tribute to the grandeur of the original. An original which, it seems to me, offers a badly needed antidote to the course of events today.

How difficult it is to rejoice in life, to sing any but songs of exile, sadness! To believe that the end of things is more than a stone's throw away; to hope that some final aggravator will not throw the stone, set off the apocalyptic. We live (faith would say we are being asked to live, God help us) in a twilit "meantime." The worst has not happened as yet, only the almost worst; with every indication, furnished daily, that worse is just around the corner. Meagre light on the human condition, paltry, diminished images of the human. Who will summon us to life? To hope?

A sorry predicament. Many stand in our midst, distraught minds closing on such words as: It is all, in sum, absurd; let us end it all.

They remind me of the mental patients, once locked away from public gaze, now walking my neighborhood, wandering my street. By no means dangerous or violent, they are infinitely pitiful. I can imagine such words as the above occurring to overwrought minds, and with good reason.

Still, I must not stop short at mere pity, or the merely pitiful. Such sorrows are images of a greater horror by far.

The truth is that citizens, purportedly in command of their wits, seated in high places, wielding great authority, are possessed by despair. Their despair passes all bounds; it is properly demonic.

Demonic weaponry, demonic diplomacy. They unseal the violence, send forth the horsemen to destroy. According to them, you and I have no future; we have no right to a future. They would gamble with ending it all.

One cannot accede to such mad conduct. We must imagine another way, pursue it, however arduous it be. Let us enter the Mount of Purgation. We were not born for hell.

2·The Quest Undertaken

Contumacy

A regal figure stepped out then
   brusque in manner blond as the sun's mane
One scar livid as a mouth cleft his right eyebrow
   another scored his breast like lightning.
  Dante do you know me? he was all eagerness
 Excommunicate reprobate I lived
Struck down my stony heart split
at last Late as a last
   heartbeat I turned to One who turned to me

 Then priests came running cursing
   They cast my bones in a pit
    they squeaked anathemas "His soul follow suit!"
 Friend believe me the ecclesiarchs haven't an inkling
Here's my true punishment stuck here
   (he struck rock with bare fist)
   two pegs in a pot hole thirty years
    the years
   I wove my will cross hatch on earth

 Please tell my daughter
   her father's saved

> *snatched by his scalp*
> *from the burning*
> *I'll see her again*
> *I'll see—*

The first soul they meet in that "other world" is, in many ways, the most spectacular. Salvation? Not a chance, humans would say. Small chance, the church would say.

But what did God say?

He says, as Dante would have it, the church can be wrong.

This sinner is chastened, gentle, thoughtful, uncontentious. He remembers his sin, he remembers the rancor of the church toward him; but he is without rancor. And he accepts the pain of his state, the delays, the humiliating purgation of his once wicked will, with a startling grace. The child emerges from the leonine pride.

Intercession is one of the works of purgatory. "Pray for me, pray for us" is a constant cry. Dante invokes a very old belief, insists time and again that the world of time and the world of the mountain are one world. In it, Christians "become what they are" (or wander far from what they are). Some come round tardily, some, as it were, borne aloft, out of their fixed pride, by hair of head, against all chance or prediction. Even their own prediction. So our sinner here. But who would not hope that such mercy as he found would attend us also?

Dante's faith. It delights in irony, upsetting fixed notions. On the one hand, faith is undoubtedly handed down, a tradition. Still, it surpasses the insight and capacity of its teachers. The church, so to speak, is in God; but God is not solely in the church. The rules of this game are for keeping; but they are also for surpassing. The God who knows the wisdom of the rules, commends them; also knows when to suspend them.

Nowhere is this game of freedom and consequence more delightfully and ardently played out than in the case of sinners. Especially those whose last breath, to all appearances, is like every previous one. Is repentance in the air? Or is their final moment only a long susurration of despair?

No one knows. Not even the church. Thus Dante.

The two purgatorial travelers have an advantage, a larger perspective. They have, so to speak, come out on the other side. There the outcome is clear, a fiction that faith tells us is plain fact. So a question can be raised, an answer offered. Were the last moments of the sinner a prelude to eternal horror? Or did his heart, hardly beating at all, run to God, in a leap that cleared the void?

Dante tells us. We can call his report a masterful poetic fiction; but in so doing we will hardly have exhausted the truth he points to. His magnificent pretension, access to the other world, reminds us that God acts there as well as here; and that our conclusions, syllogisms, systems, dogmas are there broken to bits: Shelley's "Dome of heaven like a colored glass."

We need not linger over this matter. Dante's mind was in no lockup, his feet in no lock step. He is a true believer, his mind is intact. More, his mind is alight, as to limits and overreaching, the finite boundaries of the infinite; a finitude which is both warning and glory. The church is the body of Christ; but God is God.

Lethargy

Out of the sun's fierce look
souls

hung out   yawned like poor house souls
One   jackknifed in lassitude   scarcely glanced up
mouth against thigh he mocked me
Do I hear a familiar voice
or is it a mountain goat
nosing our mountain meadow?

I looked twice   it was Messer Lazy Bones
friend of my youth
bystander   loiterer
Him I gave as good as I took

No doubt you're hanging around   for an escort worthy
of a great name   of heroic years expended?
Silence
Voice muffled   voice from an empty grave
Alas old friend   sentence is passed on me—
Conversion of heart waited on your sweet will   Now
wait out the number of years   you waited out life!

My guide stood up   brusquely beckoned me on

We are still in a kind of antechamber of reality. The drama
has not begun, audience and actors lounge about. In this world
(as in another world much like this one) reality can hardly be
borne.

The substitute for reality is—inertia.

This is not active passionate waiting, the waiting of the prophets for the coal to touch their lips, the vigils of the saints
imploring the justice of God.

Here are the lethargic; rot, a compost heap. "Who cares?"
"Who gives a damn?" The questions stun. They are in fact not
questions at all, but statements cutting to the bone; they sum
up an attitude that is close to nonexistence.

There is a waiting on grace, a waiting on God; and there is acedia, an acid eating at the soul's fiber. This delaying tactic lacks even the dignity of revolt, the malice, chance taking of the presumptuous, a casting of lots over one's fate. No point romanticizing such malaise; Satan abominates it, as do the angels.

We see horrifying photos of the tortured, the starved, the camp internees before they are led off to die; and mental patients, lost, some edge and engine of being. Such "waiting" cannot even be honored with that word; waiting for what, for whom? For—nothing, no one. This is a horrifying emptiness, as though some weight were pressing on the soul, regression, a lower order of being, unenhanced by appetite or fear or frenzy.

The lethargic are outside the circle of purgation. Nothing can start as yet. Nothing can be lost, nothing won. Pure tabula rasa.

The antecedents of this are worth pondering. Whose life ends in this dead end? What conduct led to this fate?

We are not told. No lengthy life story is offered here, in contrast to other episodes of the *Purgatorio*. And for good reason, it seems to me. The worm of lethargy not only consumes the present, turns it to dust; it attacks memory as well. It is as though these land-locked, time-locked souls have no biography, no personal or tribal history. Existence is a shrug. They crouch there, fetal, stuck in the womb of time.

It is tempting to conclude that lethargy within the life of the world condemns itself to acedia afterward. I suggest this is only part of the truth. There is also wasteful action to be considered. We see the drama played out in our own time. A moral exhaustion in the seventies follows on the moral frenzy of the sixties. Lethargy in many lives is not a continuum at all; it is a violent reaction. Some of the morally sensitive, those who risked much, who survived times of crisis (indeed contributed to its best moments), today shrug off the plight of the world. They rejoin America; a totalizing choice. Life stops there. They are stuck. One choice seems to carry everything along in its turbid stream.

The nuclear nightmare we are living through—years ago it would have moved such to a storm of protest. Now they are deflated, gone limp, on the shelf.

In light of the imperial project, spasms of protest must be accounted helpful. They are occasions of testing of will, of new strategies. They probe the weak spots in the law, lay a stress against the steel of imperial order. They are like stress weights, laid against girders; like rehearsals, war games. They point out errors, weaknesses in structures of law, order, violence. They also enable a better performance of police or army; next time.

The Unabsolved

A somber crowd sent by singing
   Have mercy on us O God in thy great mercy!
 My shadow fell on them
Their song trailed off to a hoarse cry of wonder
   You come to us
    your living body intact?

  That unbodied throng trailed after
    a span of bats or birds
   O help us pray for us
And I: *By that Lord I seek from one world to the next*
  I swear I will remember you

  One stepped forward then
Tell this among the living
   Bloodthirsty to the end I wandered the battlefield

gashed in the throat   footsore   dying by inches
I called out Mary's name   and fell

> *A cry went up from hell's throat   a gnashing of teeth*
> *"See   a single tear coaxed from his eye*
> *and this hellion is safe!"*
> *The demons mauled   made sport of my corpse*
> *They prized apart*
> *the cross my stiff arms made*
> Debris on a river bed   my bones lie scattered
> Pity then   pray for me
> that I purge away my great sins—

Misuse of Power

Out of dizzying heights and gorges
a level place   less hard on limb and will—
There   wrapt   apart   a prince in a ruin   sat one
Lord of language   bright famed   long known to me
He spoke or I spoke
or both   in concert of misery   prophecy

> *I see O see*
> *the pillars in rubble*
> *the great eagle throttled*
> *hounds of war*
> *half leashed   half let*
> *in half human hands*
> *Come faction   counter faction*
> *sour the harvest*
> *curdle the wine vat*
> *And you great godhead*
> *that hangs like a wooden*

god from our wood—
do your eyes turn forever
away in distemper
from malfeasance and murder?
see how we cower   see how we run!
orate pro nobis   gods of our inmost
guts; Gog, Magog
diplomats   pimps
appetites   frenzies—
                    orate pro nobis!
Eloi   eloi   lama sabacthani

A nother soul appears, another account of salvation. With nothing to his credit save only a single cry to Mary, this one gave up the ghost. But, according to Dante, his gesture and outcry canceled a whole misused lifetime. Violent, unabsolved, almost to the end. And yet saved, intact, resolute for the good.

Of course the circumstance is unique. If we may trust the common understanding, we are saved through the church; bell, book and candle. But this is not to hinder a larger understanding, a mysterious mercy. The outreach of God is by no means foreshortened. The earthy symbols indeed minister; but they also lead beyond themselves. They express in the gentle, usual, lowly things of this world, the infinite hunger of God; for us, for the moment of truth, for a last day which mercy names the first.

A poet appears next, a prince among the living. He and Dante find common ground in the agony of their beloved Italy, racked with war, bled white by the violence of the great.

I have not hesitated to put equivalent words about our world in the mouths of these two, a kind of Greek chorus, commenting on the follies of humans, the sword that hangs above, then and now.

The Serpent

That streak of light, that muscle
of weal and woe—
woe beyond telling
pretense of weal—
through the grass and flowers it whispered
garrote and noose
whip and loop
duplicity   diplomacy
sinister   sidelong   complicit
tantamount to murder—
what dolorous memory
that sight struck up!

Horribly it arose
the head was all smiles
a cut throat grin
as though it swallowed the world
was gorged with it

It eyed me   all eyes
Transfixed   I sweated out
the fell outcome
when sudden
as equinoctial thunder
two creatures descended

They were clad all in green
of newborn leaves
Once   twice
they clashed blunt sword blades—
The malignancy fled
like a ferret's shadow

The Entrance

We came to a portal
Stern   unbending   an angel accosted
What errand brings the living
out of due time among the dead?
His short sword clove the air
stopped us in our tracks
I knelt   seven times his blade traced
a serpentine S on my forehead
Blood   tears   fell on my face
Welcome   to dolor
to glory

We entered   The gates clapped to
like the two hands of God
ordaining ends and beginnings.

3·The Terrace of Pride

Images of the Carven Wall

The height of that mountain!
A cleft in the rock—
like blind moles or the newborn
We rode a surf of stone   it bore us
this way and that its own sharp will
The moon was down
we stepped out   sheer face of stone
and the void

That promontory wall
was carved so cunningly
it seemed the mute stone spoke

First an angel   bent to a matchless maid
you would have sworn   *hail Mary*
breathed from his lips   She in turn
spoke   or nearly so   *behold the Lord's servant*

Further   a tumultuous scene
a cart   a span of white oxen
the sacred ark   the holy city
King David   lowly   afoot
whirled   danced like a Sufi

My eyes said in despite
of sense and art   Surely the stones cry out
they are singing   the marble sings!
A third scene on the wall face   again
the marble grew importunate
vocal   responsive. A king on horseback
cavalry   spangled banners
winds bellying
A poor woman
incongruous   hangs like a leech
to the king's halter   *My murdered son*   she cries
Do justice!
On my return;   he shakes the halter.
And if you do not return?
Brusquely; *Another will right the matter.*
He spurs the horse, she moves too, rants and clings
But if you neglect   justice
how exact it of others?
He wheels his mount about. *Witch, you prevail*
And to his courtiers   *Hear this woman   her cause is just*

The guide and the poet enter this scene of purgation through a "cleft in the rock." A scene of birth, more properly of rebirth.

In the Christian view, the sin of pride is most serious of all. The Greeks agreed, though from a radically different point of view. "Exceeding the human measure," "self-inflation," "stealing fire," "storming the stronghold of the gods"—so Greek dramatists and philosophers saw the sin. And the punishment was terrible.

The method of purgation is worth noting; sin is dealt with in a parallel way on each terrace, a coherent pattern. The method expresses a profound psychological truth; our disordered love cannot be simply ordered around. We do not convert to God as punished children are said to convert to good manners.

But to come to a human measure, to play human instead of playing God, we need examples of radiant and sensible conduct; in this case, of a humility both human and godlike. This is the insight of the poet, both truthful and exact; we must imagine the human before we can attain it.

Visual art looms large in Dante; an artist of words, whose imagination took in, pondered, responded to, the great painters and sculptors of his time. He saw the message of Christ primarily as an act of the imagination; God imagines the human, in Christ his son. Then, he imagines ourselves, in the image of Christ. But not an image automatically or biologically conferred, as one receives organs at birth—eyes that see, ears that hear—organs that enable one to live in the world. In fact, the image of Christ, for most, means a purifying sweaty ascent, sin, betrayals . . .

And then, images of the inhuman as well. Which is to say, since Dante almost invariably speaks biblically, images of the demonic. The human is not a static "given." It is in conflict, its destiny is tragic. If the soul prevails, it will be at the price of a conquest over hostile forces "not of flesh and blood," tempters, seducers.

Every faithful tribe is graced with heroes who bespeak a whole tradition. At the terrace of pride, Dante draws on the widest possible history—Christian, Jewish, pagan—to show forth the wide spectrum of the holy and human. Mary, King David, Trajan the just; a triptych of truth.

Dante was fortunate in the art of his times. Cimabue, Giotto, the sculptures of Donatello—what a glory he was witness of! He can wonder, with entire naturalness, that the images "nearly spoke aloud" to him. Angelic lips all but move, vocalize. Mary "seems to answer." A rare moment in the history of art points to a rare moment for our furtive and tortured humanity.

A woman will beget God. First she must consent to him in her soul. The moment is both crux and cleft of the divine irony; the omnipotence attends on, hesitates before human freedom. Is this the method of God in the world? It is constantly his method. And the maid is a human paradigm, "choosing" the poet says, "to be chosen."

A second scene. David, king and penitent, follows afoot as the ark is drawn into the holy city. No sedia gestatoria here! He is like a primitive tribal chief, intent on serving, a wary eye out for the well-being of his tribe. In the divine presence he is brought low—where indeed he belongs. David will live long and sin with fervor and repent with scalding tears. But he will have no greater moment than this, when he walked barefoot, and even skipped and danced, in exaltation before the divine. The first of the Hassids?

Finally a pagan epiphany. In a third image, a king's progress is impeded by a poor old woman, seeking redress. The king is off on some high, unnamed enterprise; she forces herself on him. She will not be put off, will not give up, she clings like a witch to her demon; the horse's halter is a lifeline, she hangs there for dear life.

The king yields. He is no Olympian, turned to stone by delusions of grandeur. So this moment, which in the world's eyes might seem of no moment at all, an evidence even of weakness, is really a moment of glory. A king, against all custom of great ones of this earth, turns aside from statecraft to hearken to the "least of these"! For this he is remembered; for this, Dante honors him beyond measure.

The Proud Brought Low

As in a sweating distressful dream I saw them
   poor burdened souls plodding along
      enslaved;
pride of place   pride of birth   pride of achievement

     There on the first terrace
      they expunged the first sin
        purged away
   the furious inflated emptiness of the world

     It made my bones ache
     as though   aloft in stone
     grotesque grimacing figures
     knees against chin   bore the brunt
     of roof tree or ceiling—
     But these rocks were real   these souls
     all but bent double   bore their incongruous
     useless burdens
                round round
     the solitary track

     Their only prayer—
     Our Father   free to love and be loved
     praised be your name   even in this place
     The peace of your kingdom come
     (helpless we   to bring its coming)
     Angelic wills bow before you
     so may our own
     In the dread wilderness of this world
     deprived of you
     every step
     is a fool's wayward ring-around

We forgive all wrongs   Do you
also forgive us
Our strength turns to water
pour us not out   a waste

Then, the penitents themselves. Here, everything slows down, everything is burdened. False expectation is stripped, great names brought low, delusions vanish. All that remains is a sweating procession of those who are renouncing their former "life-style."

Life? It dealt only death, first of all to those who practiced it. Style? Such lives had neither grace nor beauty nor truth; let us say rather, in virtue of the outcome, they aggrandized, exploited, ground others under. They lorded it over, bore their crowned heads high. They were skilled in very human art and imperial craft. Save one. With respect to the truly human, they were ignorant as stones.

Greek myths spoke of a heroic figure, Sisyphus, condemned to push a rock endlessly up a mountain side. The contrast of his fate with the figures in Dante's first terrace is instructive, striking. The Greek hero, as Camus wrote, is a figure of plain absurdity. His task in eternity is a sign that life in time was essentially meaningless, a charade, an empty show. In hell he pushes his great rock up the mountain, it escapes him near the top, rolls down. He must eternally descend and begin all over. The cycle never ends, and therefore never really gets underway. But he pushes on nonetheless with dogged, mindless will. Beyond possibility of question his task is laid on him; the gods have appointed it. And they are turned to stone.

What a contrast with Dante's penitents! They bear a thoughtful, calm air of resignation, worlds apart from the bitter silence of solitary Sisyphus. It is not that they are guiltless, morally superior to the Greek hero. Nor on the face of it, is their punishment easier than his; they move in circles, they act out the cycle of violence and pride and blindness they pursued on earth, the death game that enslaved them. Still, their demeanor is filled with hope, they are gratefully conscious of one another, they pray and converse, comfort and confront. They clearly believe in a God who hearkens to them; they have access to his mercy.

Whereas Sisyphus bears the look of—dare one say, us moderns?—a stony defiance, matching the stony silence of the heavens. The will to defy the worst, by simply enduring; alone, if need be, in all the universe.

But the penitents are heartened by a promise of the end of torment, and glory.

A Friend Brought Low

One groaned aloud   as though the rock he bore   rubbed him raw
     he shifted the huge weight like an ox
       In that place of bondage
     he peered at me   he knew me   he called to me
         Brother mine   the chaos of the world is stilled here
   time   like a puff of wayward wind
      eon upon eon
       less than a blink of God's eye
Our egos once blared in public places

     that flourish is stilled
       death stops all throats
In this gyre we turn   beasts of burden
    beating to dust the flowers beneath our feet
     that once like fame and name   were green and gold by turn

      I said shamefaced
     The truth you grasp and give

pricks my great pride as well
But say for my instruction
how were you saved
if pride rode you to the end
to bleed and race and win
the dead leaves of the laurel?

He answered
In my city   my name
stood big as a billboard
superfluous honors
rained down   a paper storm
But I saw in nightmare
the Kingdom of mad dogs
the Bomb raining down
black rain   world's end

My family   myself
decked out   beribboned
like demon dolls
indentured to hell

To the town square I went
stood like a madman
in rags and ash
miming   begging pardon
for obeying to the jot
the law of the damned
for neglect of that good
named God

Rejoice with me!
from slavery I came
from hell   from self will
into my freedom

The Angel of Humility

An angel approached
arms open in greeting   then
        he touched   barely touched
my forehead   *The way   be easier now.*
        Indeed the way eased
                or was it rather
        lightening
        of soul's gross baggage?

        Like one who all unheeding
bears on his person   some mark or brand
                and reads   only in others'
                amusement or dread
        how awry he walks—
                I put hand to my forehead—
                That welt and wound
                assuaged   part healed!

        A choir of souls
                struck up my soul's
                breakthrough—
Blessed the poor in spirit!

The Carven Pavement

        We came then to a broad plain
                smooth as a chancel pavement
        In relief of stone or bronze
                the tools of artisans summoned
                the sins of the dead

Here penitents could read
as they dragged along
their deranging crimes

Here lay the noblest of creatures   fallen from heaven
And Saul transpierced by his own blade
And Troy   its topless towers sunk
          Here torturers   mad scientists
            degraded of mind   impenitent
and those who cast fire on the earth   crying
          TRINITY   in derision of life's Lord
               weapons   contrivances
          vainglorious   grotesque

  How praise that art   that doleful history?
      where I went stooping and peering
      the dead were dead indeed
          damned   darkly triumphant
      The originals
          dwelt in hell
Their surrogates
          warned   cried out
          Away   Away
          from that criminal track!

_____

'I said shamefaced
the truth you grasp and give
pricks my great pride as well . . . .'

I know of no more moving words in the *Purgatorio*.
    On the terrace of pride, Dante recognizes his own sin. It will
not do to stand among the penitents, even with the most virtuous
intentions, in a kind of distanced compassion, implying that

their fate, while engaging one's heart, is still another matter than one's own. No, their fate is the common fate; one must drink their cup—helplessness, solitude, public spectacle.

So Dante confesses quite simply, he belongs on the terrace of pride; his head rode too high, he had a thirst for glory.

We will hear other confessions of this kind.

Pride cannot be understood merely as an individual matter. Something more is at stake here. We must see that circle of penitence as a single circle of humanity, an image of secular history. The great are borne down with a crushing burden of evil, authority, self-will, the blind power that wreaked havoc on the innocent, the powerless.

Pride is a social crime, it demands victims, like a carnivore god. And we cry: if only the consequences could stop with the guilty! If only punishment came down on the kings themselves, the courtiers and yea sayers, the mercenaries and lackeys and client colonels! If only their delusions did not ruin other lives, declare wars, rob the sweat and labor of the poor of the earth! If they alone perished of their bullets and warheads! If they could be condemned to their gulags and slave camps! If they could be held accountable for their public crimes! Alas, alas; for the sins of the vainglorious, the proud, millions die, slow death or instant, millions never get born. The prideful threaten to turn the earth into a threshing floor, so ravaged that the living will come to envy the dead.

There are slogans, drives, myths, institutions, reflexes, loyalties, symbols that fuel the great pistons of pride, that impel the nations to violence, that seduce the citizenry, that displace and degrade the sacred, that make of violence a universal imprint. We do well to attend to these infectious spirits; they claim our very souls. And once their claim is verified, once it wins its "unconditional victory"—when this occurs repentance is unlikely. Will those who made the decision to drop the nuclear bomb on Hiroshima ever stand on the first terrace, bearing that horror on their backs, sorrowful but saved? The president said calmly after the crime: We had the bomb and we used it. Years later, he died in his bed, by every indication at peace with his soul. The military leaders whose decision coincided with his own were queried years later for their memories of the event. Not one of them expressed regret. They stood in a closed circle. We are dealing with the antecedents of hell, not purgatory.

4 · The Terrace of Envy

We took direction from the great sun
             that pours
        like God's providential heart
largesse   on wicked and just alike
          like a third eye
        the sun made our course sure

    So came   by a bare road
              to a barren outcrop
      and a multitude
              livid as living pelts
          worn inside out—
The envious camouflaged their envy
          seated along a wall of livid rock
             like beggars who take the winter sun
                or prisoners in a squalid yard
                   in deadly likeness   to the dark clay
one like another   one another   one

          I drew near   saw in a moment
why they slumped   indifferent   heedless
        of sun or moon   right hand or left
             Disfigurement wove them in one
                  fabric of misery   stitched through the
                  eyelids
        every one with thread of steel!

In the blink of an eye   the eyes were shut for good
                like a shuttered shop
        where fruits and flowers sour   fall to decay
            where souls of rats wreak havoc
            like envy's disembodied tooth—

        They rose   swayed there   a phalanx of misfortune
                between cliff and void
                    helpless   hesitant
            shoulder to shoulder
            like a blind   hydra headed worm

        Their eyes were blind   their lips
        cried congruous blessing!
        Mater Dei   ora pro nobis
        Sancte Petre   ora pro nobis
        Sancte Michael   ora pro nobis
        Sancta Lucia   ora pro nobis

        I mourned their plight
            tears of the helpless blind
                hissed on the thankless clay

    Unborn   born   twice born?
    Mary   Michael   Peter   all you saints   pray for them
        their eyes will see   the glory of God

The clay bank and the bare road and that is all. The impoverished face of nature contrasts vividly with the splendor, the great art, on the terrace of pride. Shakespeare's Iago is essentially mean of spirit, Satan's sin has its twisted grandeur.

No art on the clay bank. Is there an art of envy? We have not been shown it. Or are there exemplary people who can show the opposite virtue—largeness of heart, generosity—examples that lend themselves to art? Dante does noththink so. Envy; minimal art, no art at all.

The envious are denied even the light of day. God, we are told, makes the sun to shine on the wicked and the just, without distinction. But not here. Those whose lives have denied the goodness of God, who have turned from the sun, hoarded its rays for themselves, are plunged in darkness. The contrast is insisted on.

In the journey toward the envious, Dante and his guide depend on the sun to lead them to the land of the blind. The art conceals the art.

A terrible punishment, nearly a form of torture. The needle pushes through the eyelid; we shudder at the thought. And at a further thought. Is God a torturer? Does he pierce through the eyes of the envious, sewing them tight against the sun, effectively blinding them? We are not told, there is no prelude to this scene, to tell whether the hand of God performed this deed, or that of an angel.

Indeed, no scene of the *Purgatorio* offers us a clue as to the immediate circumstances preceding the sentence. On the terrace of pride, we do not know the instructions, no hint is offered of who hoisted the rocks to the shoulders of the guilty. We are merely shown, in one brief episode, almost a "still shot," the symbolic act of purgation; that is all. It is the same here.

Let us say, by way of reflection on Dante's method, his view of divine justice, that he is not writing a good mannered account of life's foibles; he does not come into our presence gingerly, anxious about our canons of good taste. We know that he lived in a desperately cruel time, marked (as is our own) by infamies, torture, imprisonment without trial, rancors, divisions, wasted lives.

Nor is it expedient to defend Dante as though he were a fifth evangelist. He is a poet whose insights and style can be called into question, whose taste (or lack thereof) reflects events and attitudes of his own time; events, attitudes that may well clash with our own.

That said, let me suggest that Dante is dramatizing the inmost truth of certain choices. In mortal life the prideful chose; they heaved to shoulder the burden of the superhuman. The burden was signified by the foolish amassing of money, authority misused, degradation of the powerless. Even on earth the proud did not walk free, they were incapable of receiving others as equals, they stood apart, hyperconscious of dignity, the burden and glory of office.

And the envious? On earth, they lived in the dark. They chose blindness. They turned from truth; that the goods of the earth, and the goods of the spirit, belonged to all. More, that the human response to triumph or talent or good fortune (another's, one's own, it makes no difference) is an unselfish joy. The communality of earth was a dark enigma to them, a threat. So their days clouded over, they went literally and bitterly blind. On the Mount of Purgation, they stitched their own eyes shut. But this happened long ago.

Dante, I believe, feels no call to lay at God's door the wreaking of punishment on humans. We ourselves are skilled enough in this regard; hell begins on earth. So does purgatory.

The conduct of the envious is an assault on the nature of things, hardly less serious than that of pride. The prideful would command the sun, rise to great heights, perform acts of inhuman oppression. But the envious would either own the sun, or pluck it from the sky. The dog is in the manger. He wishes neither to eat the straw, nor to sleep on it. Only to impede others.

A sour and diminishing way. The mountain turns sterile, livid before souls who could not bear with the variety and scope of things on earth. Dante places such spirits neither in a desert nor a frozen tundra; simply a clay pit, a place without beauty, grace, fecundity. Their place on the mountain is the color of blindness itself.

In ways I am by no means certain of, envy bangs its drum, finds its tempo and place, in the modern dance of death. And the tempo is echoed and taken up, drum after drum, distance on distance, as the dance grows wilder, less contained and rational—even to the dancers themselves.

Dante points up the irony of the situation in its consequences. The envious end up impoverished, deprived, even of the light of the sun; a light which they found disquieting, intolerable on earth. There, the sun was prodigal, widespread, self-giving.

Now the envious have the existence they sought all along. The earth is sour, mean, unresponsive, the sky is darkened. They must wear the coarse sacking of beggars, the indigent dead. Who says (Dante asks the question) our prayers are not answered?

Envy is finally anti-ecological.

One thinks of the chauvinism, nationalism, that afflict us. To be "number one" in the sense commonly understood is to envy others an equal access to the earth. And envy does not merely sit on the sidelines, angry and low of spirit. It arises, it is enacted in structures; there is multinational envy, military envy, cash crop envy, media ratings envy, gross national products envy. There is even skyscraper envy!

This mad nonsense, pushing up the ante, pushing our way upward in the skies, out into space, carving out sphere of influence, threatens to wring the earth dry of life. The end of the road of the envious is a clay pit.

It could be argued that the proud are blind, the lustful are blind, the hateful are blind, and so on. Dante offers the unexpected: It is the envious who are blind. The insight invites pondering—not only what the envious are blind *from* (what disease of soul, what affliction, what excess), but what they are blind *to* (what aspect of reality; what has been overlooked, sidestepped, dreaded).

A moral consequence is not the same as a physical disability. Which is to suggest that the envious are not merely blind, they are blinded. More precisely, they are self-blinded.

To envy another is to draw a steel wire through one's eyelids. Dante is savagely exact. Envy denies the light, it denies light to one's self. Then the acts repeated degrade the soul. At a certain point in this process, no outlook, so to speak, is possible. One is blind; how then look outward?

The blind, no matter which way they look, see nothing. Envy peers at both the fortunate and the victims—and sees nothing. Misses everything. Misses the rejoicing that is appropriately human, when good things befall good people. Misses the compassion due to the sorrowing, those who lose out. Like the blind in an unfamiliar room, the envious stumble about, creating havoc, emotional disorder, first of all in themselves. They rejoice with a sour joy, an inner grimace of soul, when another is wounded, put down, suffers tragedy even. And the good fortune of others? The envious grind their molars; fortune or friendship or reward or honor or wealth belong by all rights only to themselves.

Darkness indeed. We need only socialize such an outlook, to gaze on our plight; public crime, violence, amassing and hoarding of the earth—of life itself. The riches that are a vast emptiness. The possessions that lie in vault or treasury or barn, inert, of no use, of no joy. The hunger that spurs the empty to fill their emptiness with "having"; a substitute for the void which existence itself opens when one chooses death over life.

And then wars, and their outcome. The envy of the nations demands many underdogs for the sake of top dog.

The social outcome of violent envy, one to one, is murder.

And on the broad scale, the conflict of nations, the jockeying and bickering for first place among the tribes of earth? The outcome is quite simple: on the part of the victor, crime beyond accountability. For the loser, despoliation, rancor, unconditional surrender.

And then, inevitably, yet another round of violence.

On the terrace of purgation, however, souls are not condemned to an unchangeable frozen state of things, a blindness beyond healing. For that we must go literally to hell. But here, something else: healing. We are told that, one day, the iron stitches will be gently removed by the surgeon of humanity. He did not knit them there; but he will draw them forth.

Dante does not accuse himself of envy. The purgation of pride he sweats out, a prideful man. And angry he is, beyond measure. And on the terrace of lust he will be invited (an invitation with an edge) to tread the fires, along with others for whom the flesh was a baited trap. But here he stands clear, his mind is untrammeled.

And I wonder: Is it merely because he is strong, and sure of himself, and has no cracks in his armor, into which this acid of envy might seep? Not everyone is capable of everything, even of every sin; a consolation of sorts. And, in any case, Dante never was trapped in a situation where he had to look on while another snatched "his" possession, "his" loved one. Death took care of that. But Iago was less fortunate.

Anger-lust-pride. This is what we may call the Dantesque constellation. It is a dangerous grouping; and Dante may account himself lucky (he does so, in a hundred subtle ways) for attaining the first or third or seventh terrace of purgation, instead of being plunged into hell.

Such spirits as Dante are not only endangered. They are also hugely gifted. Their anger fuels a sense of justice we sometimes call prophetic or martyrlike. And the lust implies, on the credit side, a love, a capacity that burns and gives. And in the pride, stature of spirit, greatness, play hide and seek. Come out, come out, must be our cry.

Then there is another ambit: gluttony-cupidity-sloth-envy. The task here (for grace) is to awaken the dormant, half-conscious spirit, half-lost in matter as it is, like a living clam in a fused shell. In Dante's image, the spirit is blinded in a world which is all sight.

There is a hell for those who go too far, and there is a hell, or at least an anteroom of hell, for those who refuse to go far enough. There is a place for Satan, and a place, a fitting one, for those who waste, defile, rust out, refuse. These are somber thoughts, only now and then conducive to self-correction. Here is a less somber one: There are also terraces for the above described, on a mount where beatitude is at least possible. Let us say probable. Let us even dare say certain.

The envious must overcome their envy, must moreover pay for envy entertained. Along with other malefactors in parallel condition, they will achieve beatitude by the right use of a freedom which on earth they have seriously misused. They were called to be godlike, they in fact were somewhat, or even notably, less than human. On this terrace, as on others, a point missed on earth must be no longer missed. For God, to say the least, is not envious. And the envious shall not see God. Only the godlike will.

There are decrees at work here, a coherent moral universe, a rule of love so stern, so passionately in pursuit of reality, it turns the knees to water, sets the bones trembling.

5 · The Terrace of Enmity

A hymn was struck
Agnus Dei   dona nobis pacem
the wrathful loosing the knots of anger
Adam's cords

Then smoke rolled toward us
like hell's tumbleweed
—and over us and clung to us
and blotted us out
sightful   suddenly stricken
I must grope toward my brother
In hell's blear
night's black overcast
my mind fails
imaginings fall short
The foul and bitter air
hemmed us in
like spirals of barbed wire
Eyes were sealed   sight canceled
I was like the blind
restrained from injury
by compassionate hands
to the blind   blind
but to the world of sight
all sight

Then a face appeared as though masked
and a voice through the parchment lips of the dead;
Whose body cleaves the fiery fog
like a mortal being?
Walk with me I said. *Sight fails us*
we'll make of hearing a second sight

Abruptly; *Brother, I loved the world once*
my mind was tempered to serve my people
Now alas   who loves?   who pays?
whose heart builds but its own ribbed prison?
goodness is exiled, evil rides high.

I bowed my head; *Indeed the world is a desert*
barren of every virtue. But is wisdom granted
to say why? On earth, malice and goodness contend.
Some assign the springs of evil to stars and planets
their baleful emanations
Some say no, we ourselves choose.

Brother, he sighed, *the world is blind as folly's cave*
and indeed you spring from its nest.
The guilty shrug off like a scaly skin
admission of crime, run free
into ever new crime.
The heavens answer for our conduct! their cry
or genetic fault! or poisoned mother's milk!
Befouled or lucid, the springs of conduct are within
The forked stick bends to the watery source
You are free, unfree
free even to be unfree
Ask neither astrologers nor chattering divines
the roots of evil

You steer the precipitous car, you fuel its progress
You and your guardian demons

In the beginning
the soul comes forth delightedly, a little child
from its mother's body into her hands
It knows nothing, wants nothing
turns like heliotrope to this or that sensuous good
Entices, wins it.
It grows, savors each trifle, each larger good
First an apple, then a bird
then clothing, then great possessions
then guards and guns, then armies, arms
bombs begetting bombs, generations of bombs

Finally, murder is all—
form of the soul, savor of the senses, stance of the body.
The leaders ape the people who sniff downwind
the odor of apes who concoct
of the worse argument the better
Brutish conduct, silken lies!
They fuse in one tool of death
shepherd's crook and sword
blessing what should be cursed, cursing the Lord of life

In whom   in whom today
does the Savior's truth abide?
deaf as stones   leaders and led
misleaders   misled
goose step in and out   out and into
mirrors and clocks
apish   insolvent   blind—

The clocks halt   the mirrors freeze
you stand there   petrified   death's hostages

The smog of hatred rolls along, creeps into everything, claims all for darkness. The smog irritates the sight; finally it beclouds the mind, blinding as it goes.

To wage war, even the sacrosanct excuse of an invasion of territory is unnecessary. Enough that the enemy *intends* to invade, to strike first. Even the impersonal soldier, carrier of the germ of impersonal hostility, has become unnecessary, an anomaly. Soldiers in Vietnam, in Korea, in Europe, in South Sea Islands, will shortly be commemorated in tin and lead, like the quaint children's toys of past centuries. War can now be fought without them. A double abstraction prevails: enemies ignorant of one another's faces; then, enemies poised above the consoles, fingers on buttons. Distant war, distant death, no accountability, a cosmic trade off.

So hatred has its apotheosis, the earth becomes a boiling image of hell. Absence one from another, contempt for life, Promethean pride. How do we come to such an impasse?

To answer that question, we must enter into the great smog of unknowing. There, all answers are given, all doubts stilled. I think Dante had in mind the crepuscular infestation of propaganda, lies, half lies, weasel slogans, racist innuendos—an atmosphere concocted and loosened, like a lethal gas, like germ warfare. On the occasion, say, of a declaration of war. Or of a nondeclaration, when the formality is embarrassing or ill advised. But, in any case, to lay the ground for an onslaught against some offensive or unproductive or upstart tribe.

Such "weather" is available. It is the product of technique. The way one people regards another, the peaceable or hostile suppositions that govern violent times or normal times—this can be altered at will. Presto! The fog machine starts up. Citizens now have what yesterday they did not have—an enemy.

In practically every case, the enemy is, of course, a figment of slogans, fears, resentment, racism, economic gluttony. No matter. The vast majority of us, Christians among others, are enlisted—to eliminate the infamy. The war begins.

From now on crime, murder, will be the order of things. No person, however innocent or aged or ill or palpably uninvolved, will lie outside the gun sights. In the great smog the hunters drift and peer and poke and kill—their own as well as the enemy; they make mad decisions out of boredom or frenzy or lust or avarice; the war is underway.

How did the image of the filthy fog occur to Dante? Perhaps he came to understand, through his own contentious life, how war beclouds the mind, unseats the soul. Came to understand that the smog is the symbol of an inner reality, an affliction, a blindness that once brought him low.

He was a Christian from birth. As we are. We undergo the disciplines, learn the truths, are inducted into the mysteries. So we come to our majority, declare ourselves before the world as those who believe, who in hypothetical conflict or persecution would stand firm.

How untested we are, and before the "cloud of witnesses," those who dwell "beneath the altar," before the angels and "steadfast" Jesus, "enduring the cross"—what children miming adulthood! Then, thirteenth-century Florence being itself, and twentieth-century America being itself, the question arises: What occurred next in Dante's life? What occurs in ours?

He dramatizes his earthly predicament on the third terrace. Quite simply, in early manhood he was inducted into Florentine culture. It was, among other things, a culture of contention, of internecine wars. The smog machine was in high gear. Into its filth marched the young Dante. In it he was blinded, fog bound. In it, the blind killed the blind without knowing why, the blind died without knowing why. Had they known why, they could not have raised their swords. But the smog suppressed all "whys"; it muffled their hearing, lay like a gauze on their mouths. Those who died, died in a dream, a dream of glory concocted by statesmen and generals, who themselves never die in common battles of merely mortal wounds; but whose task it is to mix the stupefying drugs of glory, patriotism, immortal memory—which the immature, the befuddled, the unemployed, the expendable, the naive and unawakened and doomed thereupon breathe and die of.

Early on, Dante reconciled sun and smog, Christianity and killing. He escaped death in civil war. But he was to discover that the god of war has not only a mailed fist, but a long reach; and those who at his behest do not die quickly learn bitter ways of dying slowly. The fist opened, the finger pointed. Exile. Thus, ironically, Dante was liberated from the smog, the myth-ridden state machinery.

He lived in exile nineteen years. From the suffering and uprooting, homesickness, sense of loss, one great benefit arose. A perspective on the past. Sunlight in which he saw, as in a great distance, a filthy cloud hovering over his city, his past, his missed chances, his sins. He attained lucidity, lightness of spirit. For if he was cruelly uprooted, at a loss, without family faces and voices, that is not all. He was also—stateless.

Henceforth, Dante lived outside the radius of the smog machine. He stood liberated, in the sunlight. There he could see, not only his present predicament, but, more to the point, his former life, his lost way, his groping, his base bargaining, the violence of which he was both instrument and victim. How he had been blinded by atmosphere, laxity, day-to-day infamies, in the imperium.

In exile, loss of right conscience appeared for what it was: the moral poisoning of the world of power and violence, the climate of hell. Like the myth of the sunken machine that turns out salt forever, making all the seas salt, the Great Smogifier churns on.

May one point out that the image of black fog is one of atmosphere rather than of actual slaughter, mourning, battle? And designedly so. Dante sees the question of war as a spiritual one; psychology, poetry, faith, his skills and gifts all lead him to this conclusion. The question of war leads beyond physical violence to the question of spiritual degradation, acceptance of increasing levels of violence, silence and complicity, impact of slogans and myths, the multitudinous ways in which citizens are transformed into soldiers, Christians into killers, bishops into generals, Christianity into a sanguinary double bind, a bloody cross on the air.

In somewhat this way the image of the third terrace may have formed. Among other wonderful things, it is presented to us as the wisdom of the dead. Only the dead, we think, could be wise enough (or foolish enough)hto view war in this way. How skillfully Dante speaks for them, he almost bewitches us into thinking: The *Purgatorio* is a Book of the Dead, written by the dead. Living he too had died; the *Purgatorio* is the book of the twice born. Out of the strong came forth sweetness.

So he imagined the plague cloud, ventured into it, and was rewarded. There, imagining his own blindness, he encounters another soul who had attained wisdom, who was also unquelled. There was immediate kinship; this soul was also groping through the residue of his earthly angers, was fairly bursting to speak up. . . .

The question Dante asks is the question which the Christian in the superstate must never cease asking: Who is responsible?

The question must be pressed, even when it is met with silence. Or when the answer comes, straightfaced, insolent, negligent, in the form of another question: Responsible for what? Why insist on responsibility when there has been no crime?

You say there's been a crime? But there was none, there was only a war. And if I (the public authority) rightly recall, it was you Christians who devised a distinction which has been of immense moment at the flash point. You recall it undoubtedly. . . . On the one hand, *violentia*. By way of example, the mutual pole-axing of two simpletons at a crossroads, who thereby work off mutual antagonisms, denial of rights, whatever. And on the other hand, *vis*: the application of force by the state, whether in capital punishment or war. Not violence at all, but force, legitimate, discretionary, sanctioned. . . . For such a sacred insight, secular authority can never cease giving thanks to true believers!

But read the exchange between Dante and the not-so-lost soul. The question is insisted on, the implication is clear, even in the encompassing gloom. To ask the question is to imply that it will land somewhere, come home to roost. Who is responsible?

Of loony answers, put together in moony heads, there is no end. As Dante well notes. One can only think: His times must have been crazy as our own.

Still, sunlight pierces the smog. The soul of Dante's friend discusses these weighty matters quite dispassionately, with the insight of one long suffering and purified. You! It is you who are free, you who choose to be enslaved. You cannot pass this buck further, it stops here. On this mountain, in this suffering. If time is the cycle of the passed buck, here the cycle ends. If this world is the press where bogus bucks are printed, where junk is passed for real tender, and the cheater cheats and the straight look deceives and the pressed hand is sleight of hand— now that game is over.

The more complex the tangle, the greater the need to untangle it. The tangle: We love to see ourselves as helpless, a race of sheep, at the mercy of superminds; ruling us, spinning us this way and that, making war, making false peace. In that scheme of things, we can settle back in the smog and breathe lungfuls of pacifying gas. No god can accuse us.

We stand accused on the mountain. There has seldom been a clearer summary, a more merciless quickening and charge laid to human life. Out of death, out of deprivation and long-delayed beatitude, comes a clarity that hurts. That heals.

This clarity is also named: accountability. The Bible has a term for it: judgment. Whatever named, the activity is strictly unpopular in most circles short of purgatory. Here, on level ground, we are told that one is never to judge, oneself or others; hands off private lives, hands off public folly. One is never to point out another's sin, or submit to an accounting for one's own. "Judge not," in the sense of condemn not, hate not, play not God, be compassionate, go slow with hurt—such commands, eminently sensible as they are, are not the point. What we are in fact offered is a mutilation of the Gospel: To wit, give no pain, be nice, keep the club intact. . . Politesse forbids direct speech, so does friendship, the code, your and my "thing." Finally (and this clinches the matter), America, the culture, forbids it.

The arrangement, let it be said, works badly. Gingerly avoiding plain talk, mutual honesty, we seldom achieve common purpose, growth, political insight. The club rules hold firm, the community falls to pieces. "Free, unfree; but above all, responsible."

The marvelous, brusque monologue of the soul on the Terrace of Pride! It offers, by indirection, another name for the Mount of Purgation. It is the Mount of the Unveiling of the Romantic Elite. Accountability is in the air; first as a fact of existence (someone is accountable), then as an ethical conclusion. A finger writes: You, no other, are accountable.

Thus is the smog, a filthy relic of earthly evasion, cleared away once and for all.

6·Enmity and Love: A Dialogue

Of the Nature of Love

A stairway lay ahead
    a chant lay on our ears
    Blessed are the merciful
    and *Rejoice   you that overcome*

We walked into unknown spaces

Wondering   weeping for loss
    All I had seen   lay darkly on me
      How the world and time
        are hoarded   squandered—
        Can mortals achieve the equable measure
        of good use   letting go?

            Dante read my thought—
Hatred clings like a mold   to a rotten fruit
    the pith falls apart   stinking   worthless

    Some souls the spirit breathes on
      like good loaves
      arise   are broken   The bread multiplies   miraculous!
    Others hoard the earth   suck darkness
      from the breast of light
      But love gives itself   measureless   uncontained

The cry of love   More   Give more!
We hold out our emptiness
a beggar's pouch
The riches of love
fill us on the instant.

Visions of Meekness

An epiphany before us;   a lost child found
a woman   gaunt   sleepless   in a church door
My son   what have you done to us?   your father and I
sorrowing   have sought you.

Next: a maddened crowd   a lynching mood
a youth tossed like a rag doll   in their midst
He prayed for those murderers
turned on the Lord of heaven such look
as blocks hell's onset

I wakened   not to my old self
to a self renewed
the spell of fantasy snapped
Dante's words   like hands   unwinding a shroud
The truth peels away a hundred masks
these visions were granted   to pierce
the stony place in you
O angry man!

Visions of Sinful Anger

Then I saw in vision
unexampled anger—

the woman Procne
against all nature
murdered her son

Next
Haman the conspirator
nailed to his own gibbet
died like a shark
scornful, vicious
on that bloody board

That nightmare broke
a third
formed like a bubble
blown on the breath—
the children of My Lai
their stalwart killers
stalled above them, transfixed
in eternity's
unwinking eye

I awoke
as one
whom light
pierces to the quick—
the sun
that makes of heaven
like a delighted child
its playing field
was tossed on high—
dazzled with light unexampled
I cowered.

Dante: *When guilt eases*
the angelic presence

brings less terror
A pure delight is born

Then the light
spoke, or its spirit spoke:

The ascent is here

And my friend: *An angel*
like the stupendous sun
veiled in his own light
before the asking
directs our way.
God's prevenient love—
like one taking counsel
with his own soul:
I will do such and such
And does it.
No "we" and "they" in God
forbidding   foregoing
but single minded goodness only
Our good, his goodness.

The angel unbidden
touched my brow—
Blessed are those unstained
by sinful anger!
Then anger
a turbulent stream
infection   affliction
flowed from my breast
left me untainted   temperate

If we are alive at all, we are conscious of anger. Humiliation, a waste—part of us, the fuel of our soul. And on the positive side of the ledger, anger may imply an acute sense of justice (such and such things should not be, how can one live with them?), a finger of judgment, clear speech, rightful indignation.

In any case, it is not anger as such that is placed in question here, but sinful anger. The distinction goes to the heart of things. Dante condemns, even as he confesses, such anger as issues in hatred, revenge, ill will, the prelude to murder. We can presume he knew such moments, yielded to them. We have every reason to believe that such hatred was expended on him. But here he counsels another way, even as he yields to its command.

Unworkable, absurd, unrealistic, we know the chorus. It is the common cry of politics, the voice par excellence of this world. It is also, let us admit to our shame, the voice of Christians, in the thirteenth century as in our own. In Northern Ireland, in Lebanon, flagrantly; but elsewhere as well.

And then we have heard another voice: Love your enemies, do good to those who do ill to you.

Example and dialogue, adventures along the way, symbols, indirection; the method of Dante is rich and complex.

We stand on the terrace of the wrathful, those who have harbored personal enmities. Dante comes among them. A searching mind, restless glances. The pilgrim is not only to react to the mountain, however strange, wondrous. He is also to inhabit, know it for his own.

"O wrathful man!" The scene is a recognition. Dante meets his own demons, mockers, spirits of infiltration, bondage.

The demon of anger has claimed him; an anger he had nursed, fed on; the admission of enmity as a "fact of life." (And thereupon, inevitably, the enemy to be "dealt with"; surely one of the bloodiest euphemisms open to humans.)

The pilgrim (I am that pilgrim) is led to question things. Can mortals come to sanity? Is there a rational measure of the human—to go by, to stand by, to give by?

He has seen on the Mount of Purgation the excess open to

humans, the dark negative of the earthly scene, aglare with false promise.

Dante's answer is abrupt: Within the ideology of the world, there is no proper measure of the human. There is of course a so-called "human"; invariably a cover for the inhuman. But the seeker must go further, climb further, to reach a perspective properly divine, and therefore (the great hinge of Incarnation swings slowly open)—therefore human.

Beyond, a beyond which has become a "within," an invitation, an open chamber and school and threshing floor and banquet hall—beyond, the cry of God is heard: More! More love, more self-giving, more insightfulness, a further journey, a more painful growth and pruning. Life declaring itself, giving itself, never contained, never discouraged, never finally silenced or extinguished. We have learned something; at least something is offered to be learned. The measure of the divine is to be without measure. Is this also the measure of the human?

We are led away from enmity by examples, icons of gentleness and reconciliation. A mother loses her son on the road; she and the father seek him for days, in vain, retracing their steps, heart sick. And then they find him, like a young Solomon holding court among the wise. They do not understand, he cannot explain. The woman surmounts the impasse; a gentle reproof, entirely appropriate; then, we may presume, reunion.

A far more horrendous scene follows. The young Stephen, a deacon of the early Christian Church, has been seized. A mob condemns him to death on the spot, stones him. The youth is disciplined in the way to Jesus. He prays for those who murder him.

The visions come and go. But the guide is faithful, his speech is blunt, he is there to help disperse the chimeras, to counsel in matters of truth and untruth. The visions are true, gifts of

enlightenment. And preludes, it goes without saying, to a further
testing.

Dante would like to appear unaffected, a visitor to the terrace.
He would like to say, with a breath of relief: I have no part, or
an infinitesimal part, in the divisions and hatreds that tear at
humanity. . . And yet, the vicious circle tightens. How not hate
others in consequence of hatred? How not be silent, in face of
injustice? How do more than salvage out of the polluted age
some remnant of a better life, a better person?

Neither you nor I nor our children nor the unborn nor the
aged nor the ill. Neither the lilies of the field nor the fishes of
the sea nor harvest nor planting—
Neither the blood of the martyrs nor the tears of exiles nor the
heroism of the tortured
nor the coherent honeycomb of Buddhism nor the great vault of
Christianity nor Jews (an old story to them) nor the green
memory of Gandhi nor the rolling thunders of Martin King
No, nor the hopes which fuel us, the long savannahs of the
thoughtful, the solitudes inhabited here and there by holy contemplatives
None of these, none of these, not one, is proof, is safe.
Nothing is safe, nothing. If the plans are consummated, if the
weapons are lit, if mischance occurs.
Nothing of this will survive. We are in the hands of the ultimate
barbarians, the willful destructors.
They fear beauty because it is beautiful, truth because it is
luminous, history because it reproves their crimes, the future
because it threatens and judges.

This is what I make of our predicament. It seems to me that
the sin of anger, hatred, wrath, would light up the sky, east to
west, would dispose of all life out of hatred of life itself. Would

finally declare God a nonentity, a figment, a big bone in an ossuary. Because God's word of love is at odds with ours, his word puts us at disadvantage, his word is (short of the death of all) literally unkillable.

7·The Terrace of Sloth

Love's Exposition

In that landscape
of disaffection   of life gone awry
of the errant   the burdened   the self blinded
I pondered
Can love   be the moving principle   of the stars?
If love be all powerful   root   flower of all
how then does love fall short   evil
make havoc of fair hope?

But Dante; *The law of love is within*
as life in a living tree
Praise?   blame?
the tree bears what it bears . . .

Our case differs by far
in us arise
counsel   reflection
These winnow our loves   guilty or good
Our control   freedom—
On these the whole matter hinges
to love   to hate   to love this   to love that
to weigh   to discern

Therefore
the discipline of the mountain
its tasks   delays
its purifying ascent
Here the slack will
is drawn taut
Love of the good
purified
The heart   human at last
godlike at last   fit to see God!

The Terrace of Sloth

Weary in limb and mind
toward midnight we dozed
a gibbous moon   made the stars scarce
suddenly   a throng
broke   silence
eerie footfalls   ululations
My hair stood up
A ghostly cavalcade
a marathon of thin boned dead
hurried past   like wind driven leaves
their voices
ghostly bells   echoes of passage

Fainter than day's solid images
between dream and waking
they came   passed like shadows   vanished

I saw
hands of scholars   boneless as ribbons
Saw   faces of monks   whose boredom
death lifted like death masks
Now they ran   eager   on the spoor of life

        I saw
those who yawned   years away
        in   ivory towers
    fixated in airy speculation
    They pressed forward urgently
their eyes hot as rabbi Christ
        after the wine of life

The dead? I marveled   These are the dead?
    these swift paced spirits   alight   alert at midnight
            while the living
        drift   slow of pulse
            in heady or horrid dream

        I heard half heard them
    ghostly bells   vocables of birds
        a phrase   a word

Mary who hastened   into hill country—
and   *Michael of the swift sword—*
again—*You saints   your time made good—*

        They were gone   My eyes
    closed round them   my arms
gathered them in like birds or bells
        or ghosts of these
        in dream

The once slothful do not repent of their sloth by suddenly becoming "efficient." They are no more efficient, in fact, than those who heft stones or grope about in blindness, or lie prone on the earth.

In any case, efficiency could hardly be called the hallmark of purgatory. In this, purgatory is like heaven and unlike our world, which more closely resembles hell in its vain charade of "moving things," "getting things done," generally in an atmosphere of noise, confusion and emptiness.

The once indolent. One thinks of escapists, those who dodged responsibility or rotted away in acedia; all who shrugged off the discipline of prayer; those who settled for a mediocre marriage or friendship; those who hid out like good Germans in time of tyranny. Also the tolerant, to whom any religion—imported or indigenous, trivial or ancient—is good as any other. Also those who claim to know the world, to know that "nothing changes," that "there always have been wars, there always will be," that "idealism is foolish, useless, a stage—you'll get over all that," who use this so-called knowledge to push a pernicious fatalism. All these, Dante places on the terrace of indolence.

Such souls are not suddenly called to become efficient. In fact, purgatory itself is a highly inefficient series of useless works and deeds, of nonworks, even dead stops. Some souls hurry about (as here), we are not told where or why; some are transfixed, immobile, as the envious or avaricious. It really makes no difference, since the purpose of each activity or passivity is by no means attainable through good works.

These have, in fact, nothing to do with the meaning of purgation, which lies within; a matter of imagination and soul, a change of heart.

Which is to say, the souls here are aided—by symbolic acts, prayers, mime, drama—to imagine their healing in order to bring it about; or better, to have it brought about.

They are called to become godlike, insofar as this may apply to creatures. To imagine the perfectly human through activity which goes counter to their former more or less guilty imperfection.

Now they do what they were really doing on earth, if only they had understood (as in the case of the envious, who wandered about blinded to reality). Or, as in the plight of the slothful, they do what they refused to do on earth. They bestir themselves,

renew their energies, confess God, praise "the dearest freshness
deep down things."

Praise, gratitude, activity properly godlike. This is what the
indolent refused on earth. Now they hunger for the realities they
once despised.

Probably Americans would not be inclined to see themselves
appointed to this terrace. We the indolent? But we are the most
industrious of people, we create, work, earn as we go. Indeed
we are inclined to take a dim view of the indolent, to stigmatize
them, even to banish them. Clearly those belong in servitude
who cannot make it in the great lottery of the consuming society,
where all are urged to play, where all must pay up; and where,
of all who gamble, very few win.

Thus the myth of virtuous work, and work as virtue, is re-
hearsed, dusted off, played like a grooved record, droning on in
the darkness. Our national virtues, presumably exempting us
from the terrace of indolence, do not, for all that, grant access
to the beatitude of the zealous. We avoid one excess, not by
exercising the contrary virtue, but by falling into a deeper ditch.
In this case, intemperate activism, furious obsession with money
and pride of place, distraction of mind, envy. One might ponder,
for instance, that a people who create and maintain a military
establishment capable of blowing the earth to hell, can hardly
be called indolent. But to what end? Words fail.

Or perhaps we have come full circle after all, and the Pentagon and its assorted wonders is a monument to precisely the
vice of the fourth terrace: a towering indolence of spirit, indif-
ference to human fate, including our own, handing over of the
"good of intellect" to moral dwarfs. They are blind, we are
obedient; in such a division of gifts there can be no divided
outcome, all are doomed.

But in such reflections we are dealing with the vices proper to
hell, not purgatory.

The electric energy of the fourth terrace is indeed no mere
spasm of reform or effort to recoup lost time. Least of all a

place where the benighted are instructed in the virtues of good
puritans. Here, rather, one may ponder the measured urgency
of soul proper to grace itself. Which is to say, faith and works,
rightly understood, are here joined as halves of one soul, two
aspects of the body of Christ. A fleshing out of the scene of
hurrying spirits would evoke other images of holy energy: the
urgency, even abruptness of Christ as he moves toward Jerusalem and his passion. Also the apostolic journeys of Paul, the
bone clean economy of genuine contemplatives, in speech, in
quiet. In any case, no beating about, no waste, of time, of words,
of main energies and intent.

I set down these reflections in a priory in the mountain country
of Vermont. One senses that the monks are not acting out the
excesses or defects of the terrace of purgation. They work and
pray diligently, seem at ease with one another and outsiders,
each with his own soul. They receive me simply as a brother
whose nonviolent concerns are theirs also.

I feel at home; there is a sense of drawing up to a common
hearth where friendship is warmed, tales are told, the common
cup is passed. Time for one another. Time for God. An austere
good sense. *Conversio morum*; mending one's ways. A style comes
through; not bastardized chic, but simplicity: stones, wood,
paint, inconspicuous buildings gracing the hills, allowing mod-
esty its shine, finish—like a smooth stone rubbed in the palm of
the hand, left where it was.

8·Evil and Earthquake

Vision of Evil

That time of night it was   cold upon cold
    the moon   an icy bucket   poured on earth
        cold lingering light
            The soul cringes
in cold limbs   the heart's beat slows
    night's garment stiffens like a shroud
            Then
    we most resemble
        in limb and look
        the rigid wide eyed dead

Icy with sweat   I dreamed
        a half human figure
    in limb and look deformed
        color of spleen and envy
            fangs   claws
                hinting violence
                hinting depravity
        as though the body like a camouflage
            hid worse things within

            Like Blake's dew eyed innocent
                I gazed and gazed

      then desire   that artful healer
     worked its befuddling wonder—
  The toadlike horror yawned
     jaws slackened
     hide
     fell away like a limp gauze
A princess   a living jewel   stood there

  The gaze that made the vision
     gave it voice
        She sang—
Beloved   my body
   is lotus and ambrosia
     eat   drink of me
She yearned toward me

  When alert to that leeching lover
  my friend sprang between
on the instant   rent those lying garments
     the stench of truth
     the stench of death
was my awakening

       Three times he said sternly
    I called you
    Come!

Dante sleeps on the mountain journey; and, life being what it is, he not only sleeps, he dreams.

And what a dream! It shifts about, it is filth and ecstasy, the forbidden and beloved, the call of the flesh; finally, the intervention of conscience—in the nick of time.

Dreams, we are told, mark transitions of soul. If we are lucky and moderate, they help us from terrace to terrace, level to level of life, a taste of things to come, a chance to ready ourselves, to brace, reduce shock. But if we are so unlucky as to be subjects, not of the sensible, rational way of the world, but of a call to rebirth—then we commonly undergo, not dreams, but nightmares.

The phantasmagoric, terrifying shapes and images, beasts and near humans, the souls divided, death rampant! Visitants like Dante's would like to have us eat them alive, or would eat us alive; roughly the same thing.

The dream of Dante is overtly sexual, primordial, a love of death.

The dream is alluring. It is a drawing aside from primary good, and consequent loss of that good. The good is simply God. Once the good is let go, we are no longer in effect on the mountain at all, no longer in holy purgation. No longer, if we are to trust our guide, in the real world. We are in hell, where the "good of the intellect" and the good of the world are lost.

How is one awakened from this self-induced stupor? According to Dante, a woman is on guard against the demons; conscience perhaps, grace on watch, the feminine, guarding against an uncontrolled sensual drive.

The dream figure comes on, ugly as sin. The first part of the dream is not an enticement at all, but a transfixing horror. (We do not get what we want in our dreams. Normally we get what we need; what we need to know, to be warned of; that other side of things, conscience as censor.)

In any case, the first portion of the dream is a midnight stalker. She comes to remind that we are indeed fallen among the fallen, to shake up our sloth, to show a true image of our worth and world.

The first stage of the truthful dream is thus a figure out of Bosch's hell, or St. Anthony's temptation, or Christ's struggle in the desert. A truthful image; but not yet everything. For there is not only the dream to be reckoned with, but the dreamer; and what does one make of the dream that says: Come, I am reality.

The vision is, to say the least, hardly neutral. Its presence calls for a response; it is there for us, our sake.

So far, the dynamic is all on the part of the dream; the world as besotted, hideous, unhealed. It makes its case by simply standing there. Its message is its form; it says: Come. If you dare.

And the dreamer? He is, by definition, not awake; which is to say, in thrall, captive, indebted, at the mercy of spiritual powers. He is fallen, who is subject to others. This is the first act.

Then ever so slowly (or ever so quickly) the dreamer begins to love the dream.

A dream image holds us in the palm of its hand. Then the hand turns over; the gesture signals the release of great energy. It is not merely that we "get used to" the thralldom of demons. Dante presents us with something more. As love is said to transform the beloved, so here love of the demons transforms the demons. They were formerly a horror, an abomination, the necrophiliac parody of life. But desire confers on them, like a gold cope on a stinking corpse, an altogether transformed aura. These powers, principalities, dominations, demons, parodies, now appear as friends, lovers, counselors, beckoners, gurus, cherishers, partners, stimulators, teachers, advocates.

The demons wait on desire before they possess us. There is courtesy even in hell, though it is tactic rather than soul; eager and wakeful, they await a nod before moving in.

So desire created a new, utterly deceitful dream figure out of a truthful and simple one. Desire did this, and so strengthened the grip of the dream. Now the dreamer cannot break the dream, does not want to.

A dream is a dream precisely to the degree that it reproduces, mimics a conscious state, a state of "normalcy," a state wherein the dreamer can declare: I am I. I am in command. I am capable of rational judgment, of conscientious activity. I am in the power of no evil desire or drive. . . . Or, on the other hand; I am utterly helpless. I can do nothing. My fate is in other hands than mine. . . .

Let the dreamer gaze outward on the world, the fantasies go on. The times are not so bad, a few bombs are not so bad, prisons and ghettos are not so bad, to every lifetime a few necessary wars, a system which allows religion such wide scope cannot be bad. . . . Or the fantasy induces fixation, helplessness, at once selfish and despairing; religion sublimely indifferent to the world's people, or an empty activism, joyless, self-consuming.

In such ways does the former demon become the present beloved, the beloved named death.

I write this in the garden of a Jesuit novitiate; sunny dream-ridden southern California. More and more young men find us a goodly company and apply to join us. Novices are plucked open-eyed, voluble, out of the mainline Jesuit universities. They come here to pray, spread their wings; the atmosphere is of books and barbs and bonhomie. But when the subject of the Bomb comes up, as it does frequently, the air suddenly thickens with cold war clichés. One could hear the same talk at any moderate right of center common room in the nation.

Practically no one has read Gandhi or Nhat Hanh or Tolstoy or Martin King. The Gospel, one thinks, has been scanned once and shut again. I come in their midst as a rather exotic myth, no one reads my books or knows my history, beyond a few lies of Timespeak. Most discussions on the Bomb (and, therefore, on Christianity) start at dead sea level. I have an impression of being considered well meaning but naive.

There is no urgency in the air. It is a dream within a dream. You buy the dream, you enter the dream, you pronounce vows to foster the dream, the dream takes you in its arms.

Then the arms fold round you, the body presses you down; you are half-suffocated by now, only half-alive; but still, the dream, the dream, the act of love:

Thou shalt not kill.

It is a voice like thunder.

Thou shalt not kill, thou shall not bomb, thou shall not invest, thou shall not consume, thou shall not be silent, thou shall not debate how many should die.

Thou shall not hide out, thou shall not equivocate, thou shall not befog with dead expertise, thou shall not huckster dead ideas, . . .

If the Jesuits are to deliver us from the world, who will deliver us from the Jesuits?

I set these words down, facing westward, near a stone wall of warm boulders. Over the wall the magniloquent flowers pour, the hummingbirds stitch and weave and dart.

Who will tell us the truth, who will awaken us, who will free us from the walled garden, the dream, the prison of narcotics pushers and users, ourselves? Who?

Something, someone awakens us.

We tumble half-awake, discovered, shamed, angry as sin. It is—grace. The face is veiled, the name is spoken. We half remember the dream, a brimstone smell, a flash of nakedness. But in that instant, we know the true name of our beloved, our whore, our world, our bargain, our bed. It was—death.

And perhaps also in that moment, we learned the name of the elusive gift, the unveiler, the unmasker, the opposite. I hope so. Let it be so.

Earthquake

That foul dream receded
    we moved   hastened onward
when under our feet
    Earth shook like a drum head
My veins turned to ice

In that house of the dead   mortality shook me
        head to foot
Our mountain swayed and groaned
then
as though catastrophe
    engendered triumph
      a hymn sounded—
    Glory to God in the highest.

We stood there like shepherds of old
    on whom the skies rained down
good news of the Newborn

And all about   the multitudes of the mountain
    befogged   burdened   shackled
      blinded   put to silence

—as though the last day's trumpet
    broke on their ears—
      transfigured stood
  steeled themselves   sang like singing birds
     Glory   Glory   Glory

I think   what we suffer in this life
can never be compared
to the glory   as yet unrevealed
which is waiting for us
All things
eagerly wait on God
Creation retains the hope
of being freed   like us
from its slavery
to enjoy the freedom and glory
of the children of God

From the beginning until now
the entire creation   as we know
had been groaning
one great act   of giving birth
And not only creation   but we
first fruits of the Spirit
we too groan inwardly
as we wait
for our bodies   to be set free
For we must be content
to hope
that we shall be saved
(salvation is not in sight
we should not have to hope   if it were)
We are not saved as yet
We must await
with patience—
The Spirit   comes   to help us   in our weakness

(Romans 8: 18–26)

9 · The Terrace of Avarice

No end of sorrow   of labor   We climbed and climbed
    came forth   a stone outcrop—
This parody met our eyes—
      a scene of random death
      as though hell fire overhead
        rained slaughter on a city

    Then I heard   that field
all amurmur   like monks or bees
    monks at orison   bees mounting a cloud of flowers
      My body is flattened to earth
      O quicken me in accord with your promise . . .

    I drew near   one soul lay there
      inert as his own last day
        arms   feet   pinioned to brute rock
    Do you lie there brother   spurning heaven's mercy?
    Say rather   heaven turns from me   he mourned
      his words deflected   muffled—
I was the shepherd of Rome   treacherous avaricious
might well have chosen   for pontifical name
    Judas the Second

    What a lie my life became! On that throne
      I squatted like an idol
    fused in the furious belly

where Caesar's gold   hardened and cooled
a dumb calf's image
The calf worshipers groveled
The calf grew to a great bellowing bull
that rampaged   ravened in Saint Peter's fold
Cut to knee now   flattened to dust
by that toreador whose sword—
(he sighed a dusty sigh)
On earth our tongues like tongues of dogs or toads
sifted the filth for carrion wealth

Now the karma decrees
full turn of the wheel
In bitter consequence
we live out what we loved
hostages bound over
for ransom   for rebirth

And what of those others
non popes   non caesars—
graft takers   drifters!

They littered the ground like leaves
part ashen   part green
whom the lofty many tongued tree of heaven
curses and mourns

A whole summer's
offscouring
they lamented there
that lost chance   that god and earth forsaken
ground   They clutched and let go
let go and clutched   handfuls of dust and ash
traced with illiterate hands and feet
in dust and ash   the hieroglyphic of loss

No escaping the ironies of Dante. On the terrace of avarice all are folded in the mercy and discipline of the church. They seek for intercession, they lament, cry for mercy. A communion of near saints defines them, a kind of near beatitude.

Here, too, the penitents weep for shame. They let go the deceitful riches that have made a lie of their lives. And in this unlikely place Dante comes on a pope; prostrate like all the others, shamed and weeping. Dante, son of the church, knows well that the church is a sinner, not much better (at certain times, in certain members) than those she presumes to shrive and heal.

There are popes in hell, there are at least two in purgatory. This one addresses him, confesses, weeps before him; another he only glimpses in a crowd.

In high and low alike, avarice is a stalemate. Therefore the penitents are stretched on the earth they once misused. Avarice moved them mightily, they were world movers. Now the clocks are stopped; so is the heart, so are its movements, appetites. They lie inert, victims of gravity, the pull of gold.

But gold does not sweat or weep. And they sweat and weep. The heart is not merely stopped in death, it is changed. A change of heart has made of their hard hearts hearts of flesh.

There is no more sorrowful, insightful passage in the *Purgatorio* than the monologue of the avaricious pope. On his throne he "learned what a lie life was." It would be inaccurate to speak of cynicism; it has no place here. What he learned was that gold, to which the throne gave easy access, also paved the road of betrayal, the road that nearly brought him to hell. He walked that gleaming pavement in great pomp; and so he betrayed, like Judas, who loved money more than the Lord.

Popes come and go, and the recumbent figure, sweating out his sins on the austere mountain, seems like a relic of another age. Popes come and go, they are guilty or guiltless today also; but, if guilty, not of avarice. Indeed, they live like Spartans or prisoners of conscience; some would say, prisoners of the Curia.

But the historic sins of the great schism or the high renaissance are committed no longer; that tainted drama is long over.

What is not over, what will not be over until the final trump it seems, is the almighty march of the dollar. Creation itself is stamped with Caesar's superscription: Time is money, the earth is money, work is a commodity, goods and services are devalued, the stock market is bullish or falls to knee. How many know the earth, how many love or reverence the earth? We know something else, we value something else: the buck, fast or slow, hoarded or squandered.

More souls, Dante tells us, are crowded on the terrace of avarice than on any other. The avaricious outnumber the proud, the hateful, the gluttonous, the lustful.

Is this merely a reaction of Dante to his mercantile culture? I hardly think so. He is pointing to a wider issue. Every imperial arrangement, from the bickering first families of his native city to our own bickering superstates—every such system pays its tribute to the merciless face (it is always the same face) on the coin of the realm.

Religion also. The pope who once stood at the head of a majestic procession, along with the powerful of this world— gentlemen, clerics, state officials, warriors, the guarantors and protectors of privilege—the pope is brought low. With a difference; from his high and holy eminence, he has fallen lower than the others.

He was ornament of the high culture, surrounded by the armament which protected his dignity and office.

From Peter the fisherman to this? From the prophets to this? From Martin King, Gandhi, to this? In a setting of worldly pomp and glory, one is radically incapable of imagining such beginnings, such fidelity, austere lives, lives of risk, lucid speech, martyrdom. The symbolic gesture, the living example, the radiant light that draws all eyes and hearts! After such deviant centuries, we can hardly imagine the lowly rabbi of Nazareth; hardly measure the gulf that separates his way from ours.

Prayer of the Penitents

Then I heard a prayer
Mary   friend of the poor
how poor yourself   a stable floor
rank with droppings of dumb cattle
sheltered your newborn son

Moved beyond words
Who I thought
Calls on God's mother and maid?

One cried unprompted,
You hear our common prayer
as long as daylight favors

alas night falls
another mood descends
In cavalcade   the damned
ride our eyes roughshod
Souls like leaves or dollars
flare in hell's bonfires
toss in hell's crosswind
Mockery   reproach
charge the black air—
Simon Magus   Sapphira   show us your
spurious merits   your
faked credentials
And Judas   can it be
gourmet taste of silver
or jarring gall stones
make your guts rumble?

An angel's hand on my forehead
healed in a moment   the S branded there

Blessed are those who thirst
I was like a climber
who jettisons useless gear
nearly weightless
my footfalls sprang

In those inaccessible reaches
a friend   a poet
joined us
Emboldened   sorrowful
My heart stock still
I dared question

How did avarice find place
in so noble a life?

Not avarice   but its opposite
no virtue at all   but subtler vice

In the fool's mirror of my mind
I stood
loose lipped   prodigal   lackluster
sowing folly like chaff

I saw the vision Christians saw
saw
heroic visionaries
who tasted for reward

the auto da fé   the parrot's perch   the blows of thugs
I said yes   with half a heart
my no   lacked all heart
money   covert praise   shelter   I gave and gave
so   kept at distance
the bitter outcome
of "come   follow me."
I played out on a fish line

the baits and lures   that never took their fish
fishmanship   not fishing
Christendom   not Christ

You see the outcome
forty years   sweet worldly life
four hundred years
trudging the fourth terrace
as though the circle could   by hook or crook
be squared

I died badly
but not so badly
that mercy's long outreach—

He paused there   arms outstretched to heaven

There is a faint wiff of hell in Canto 20.

Their days, we are told by one of the penitents, are all entreaty, praise, songs of faith expunging the old lusts. Then night comes on, another mood arises among the prostrate, a mood of mockery and derision. Do bad dreams bring it on? Are these voices, which mock the eternally lost, heard also in hell?

It all seems strangely out of kilter. Then one pauses, perhaps because Dante so rarely strikes a false note. Is he saying something about "being not too holy"? Only in heaven, we are told, is there no dark side of the soul; and we are not yet in heaven, by far.

So the souls praise and sweat and cry out by day; and by night they deride the fallen, the lost. Something here disturbs, an unexpected truth. I would not choose to mock even the lost. I find it difficult to conceive that such derision would give pleasure to God. Are the souls in purgatory thinking to win favor?

Perhaps something different is implied. If the Mount of Purgation is an image of the human journey toward God, and the end of the journey is not yet reached, then along that journey, and even among the purged, moral conduct will have its flaws. Pathos enters. A double spirit prevails. Or, if it does not prevail, at least it is in the air. A double rhythm, self-contradictory, even; one conduct, attitude, under the light of the sun; another under the moon. And this too is an image of our state, which is not different in kind from theirs—both lightsome and crazily lunar, one person by day, another by night. How did Paul say it? "I sense in my members a double law. The things I would, I do not; things I would not, I do. . . ."

As there is an opposite virtue to avarice, so there is an opposite vice. The vice mimics the virtue; prodigality, wastefulness, in the sober dress of largeness of heart, generosity. Deep waters indeed.

Dante meets a poet and friend who lingers on the terrace, not because he hoarded life or gold or talent, but because he wasted all these. The original perhaps of the near-hero so dear to moderns. This one's epitaph might be—"Almost." Almost of stature, almost heroic; the near-hero leaves the taste of "almost" in the throat, an ache, a sense of something missed. The piercingly accurate touch of Dante! A sense of having missed life, missed goodness, missed what might have been—thus goes the story of his poet friend.

To say that all is not lost is to say little enough. Closer to the truth, all is not won; not yet. This poet in purgatory was an ardent camp follower of the saints. He ministered, admired, emulated—and fell short. He hoarded life; he kept a secret that did not belong to him, like a purloined jewel. He was, he tells us, a Christian in everything save the public confession. Everything but. But in bad times to be a Christian *in petto* is not enough. The choices narrow.

And then what does one do? God help us.

10. The Terrace of Gluttony

The Way of Thirst

Exhaustion
    the middle march
        we trudged on
I thought of that Samaritan woman
    her heartbreaking quest for truth
A living water Christ said *would heal thirst forever*
She looked at him blank eyed

And I was she
    throat parched   mind a desert
        dragging myself
through the lying mirage of the world

    My friend and I
like two disheartened men   on Easter evening
        deceived in hope
           raked by death's harrowing
    whom the Lord joined   companionably on the road

        A third walked with us
           The insight of the dead
        sensed my thirst
Why did the mountain shake to its great root?

He began   *We penitents*
dwell outside changeful law
rain   snow   fog   earthly weather
None of these stains the serene crown

More. The discipline of the mountain   a law unto itself
suffers no intervention
no intruding novelty

The base of the mountain may tremble
its forests flatten in gales
its flanks shudder in equinoctial storm
Here never

With one exception
Creation groans in travail
for the birth of God's race
Our Himalaya shakes
its voice a wild Shekinah
the "gloria in excelsis"
you marveled at

Marvel! my liberation

In life   divided from myself
longing for God   bound
in nightmarish slavery—
For this was I fastened
five hundred years
to the great groaning wheel of purgation

The Tree of Abstinence

Rooted in rock cranny
like claws in virgin rock

a munificent tree
blocked our path
like a cloud of gold
tethered to stone
verdant   fruitful
out of reach!
Wild odors crowned it
an aureole   on a saint's brow
Touch-Me-Not   its name
like a ban in paradise

and around   and around   and around
a parabola of ghosts
skinny as spiders   nervous as ants
approaching   receding
a wavering scarf
tightening   loosening
never possessing

They were like mummies in rotten sacks
once plump with wheat   now leaking
a dust of wheat

In those ravaged eyes
(sockets where the soul shone through
like reddened coals
receding to their black)
I read a strange peace

Desire   control
arousal   conformed will—
Like coals blown hot in prevailing winds
cooled in God's delay
their eyes yearned upward
their hands forebore

They peered at us
like eyes of Dachau
eyes of Leningrad's siege
lives whom death engorges
after long self waste—
only here   a strange reversal

We lived on fat of the land
robust   sleek   robber barons of time
> *pure appetite   impure excess*
> *now*
> *captive to merciless mercy*
> *we thin down and down*
> *to the needle's eye*
> *the crotch of rebirth*

> *Pray for us who exceeded*
> *modest human measure*
> *ate   ate   ate*
flora   fauna
> *wreaked*
> *havoc on natural order*
> *ate   ate   ate*
> *oil and oil slicks*
> *diamonds dredged by children*
> *subterranean gold grimed*
> *with sweat and blood of slaves*

> *Rough shod we rode*
> *the flayed backs of the poor*
> *our bellies big as a world bank*

> *Manic collectors   auctioneers*
> *we ate with eyes' lust*
> *drama   decor   found objects*
> *finders   keepers we*

Finally like cannibals
            we hunted humans
                Rampageous appetite
        bartered skins and souls
                    domineering   commandeering
squads   squadrons   air force   ground force

        We died
                gorged as pythons
            with the dead weight world
        Mercy like an emetic
        made us sick   Our arses
            stink with lees of crime
                Death dumped us out
            dustmen on a dust heap
                meager shadows now—
                    skinny ghosts
            devalued   deflated
                on earth named
Midas   Croesus   Rocky   Dupont   Ford—

        We cast no shadow
        cast no vote
            no proxy mercy

We die of what we fed on
    live on what we lack. . . .

The Second Tree

            Quick   Quick   Quick
        the voice of penitence
        was like a whip stock

                whose S   large on the air
                    inscribes our guilt

In a grassy place   a gentle reprieve
        we came on a second tree
all alight   as though for children's Christmas
                    fruit flowers   trifles
                        glowed
                like the tips of tapers
        and the leaves of the tree   were clamorous
                    as a tree of peacocks
                    eyed with peacock glory

The souls pressed forward   backward
drawn by appetite
reproved by the tree of tongues—
I am flower of that parent stock
your mother plundered
Now your divided wills
desire   abstain
refrain   reach out
until a healing grace
touch you and me
and I may kiss your lips
wholehearted as a heart in love.

T he travelers encounter not one tree but two, images, we are
told, of self-control, abstinence. The fruit is there, but just out
of reach; creation is subject to a law of measure, limits. And
these, having been violated on earth, are vindicated here.

     There is a kind of artful reenactment of the first days of the
world, as the myth of Genesis tells it. On the mountain, pen-
ances, restrictions. The original command—"Of every tree you

may eat, but one"—is now honored by obedience, as it was once honored in the breach.

We are told that questions of sin and guilt are befogged today, rendered questionable by new data, theories, experiments; as well as by the simple facts of life. Those facts are far from reassuring. We have gotten rid of God, but the news brings little comfort, for most of us would hesitate to proclaim that we have found a better master, or are better situated for having none at all. We may be sinless people, in our own eyes; but we are also victims, whose fate it may well be to witness the end of the world, to be part of that end, its passive tinder and fuel.

Who is our God? The technicians play God, a different matter altogether. They pluck the forbidden fruit, they take us hostage, they initiate terror in the world—all of this under the sober, austere sign of "progress," "defense," or similarly inspired babble.

Shall we call the sin one of gluttony, or envy, or anger, or pride? Indeed, a false clarity is worse than none at all, as Dante would be the first to assert. The point being not to catalogue sin, but to admit its existence—in us, as in Dante. Following such a momentous breakthrough, it may also be of interest to test our understanding against an ancient one, resumed, vitalized by Dante. Indeed, our sins glut the world with anguish, foreboding, regressive conscience, enslaved churches, inert citizens, destroyed heroes. Was ever such hunger for death so flagrantly fed?

Bait as we are for imperial appetite, victims of spurious myth and inane morality, we are hardly apt for the creatureliness and simplicity of Dante's penitents. Are they not, living or dead, children of a simpler age, of a simplified ignorance? More, could they not count on a measure of control over their destiny, a control which technology and the superstate have snatched from our hands?

As to gluttony, perhaps the sin and the penance once made sense. It may indeed be true that in some distant, sane world fairly sane folk once sinned against right measure, made amends, were set right—the tree of the universe standing as both judge and advocate. Thence they passed to eternity, where the "good of the intellect" orders and enlightens all other goods.

Things may have been so, once. But who is to accuse us of sin today, if in the midst of shattering turmoil, the threat of the end of time and this world, if amid confusion of soul, we made our way as best we might, pluck what fruit we may, steal where we must?

Here as elsewhere in Dante, sin cannot be considered merely as a personal matter. The gluttons are not absurd fat men at table; they are thieves, bribe takers, tycoons. Funny or tragic or broken by life, they slog away, salvaging whatever good has survived in themselves. But their segregation in purgatory is by no means meant to inhibit a larger understanding. Here as elsewhere on the mountain the social and symbolic aspects of the fall from grace are part of the drama of redemption.

Gluttony. Each of us is debtor to the universe, we pluck in measure, beyond measure, what is ours, what is not ours, appetitive beings in a giving world. But the tree we take from, within or beyond right measure, is the universe itself. And we will answer for it. And our rape of the tree, or our restraint before it, are images of our attitude toward life itself, including our own.

Of every tree you may eat, except one.

That one, that forbidden plenitude, all the more enticing because off bounds—what does it mean?

We might note in passing that, in Dante's poem of the mountain, two trees, not one, are off bounds. The ante, so to speak, is up.

In retribution for the sin of Genesis, which each penitent has repeated in other times and places, each must pass by, without touching, tasting, consuming, two trees—unutterably beautiful, beyond grasp or possession. Repentance is sterner, more circumscribed, than the original command. The law once broken is not canceled or revoked; indeed it returns doubly stern to haunt the violator.

There are signs in parks and gardens: Keep off; warnings interminable not to trespass, enter, cut corners. . . . It is depressing, as though the rich owned the earth and the rest of us were locked in macadam compounds. A perversion surely, a mockery of the intent of God in setting limits to cupidity, invasions of appetite. What a relief the Genesis story is, with its largehearted gesture, a simple restriction placed on only one good thing, one tree.

By forbidding a single good thing, every good thing is protected. I do not know why this is so. I do not know why every good thing is not in the nature of things, good for us. Nor why the urge to overstep, to try the limits, to disobey, throws out of focus all the wondrous good things already free and at hand. Or why once the bounds are passed, and the forbidden good is tasted, all former joys seem tainted.

Every self-proclaimed revolution is shadowed by such questions, such realities. As though in a desert place (practically any place in the world) as pilgrims make their laborious way toward a promise, the buzzards should circle overhead, with their sure instinct for the presence of death.

Why this is so, no one seems to know. Experience teaches only one thing, unsatisfactory to pilgrims—that it is so. We need a proclamation—"Keep Off"—to keep us from playing God, going too far.

And this hoarding of the world is the plainest figure I know for the sin of gluttony. It is a cruel caricature, the opposite of the providential One, the Heart of largesse, the God who, being free, gives freely to all.

11·The Terrace of Lust

Purgation of Lust

We turned and turned   on the stone spiral
        Zeal hurried us on
              Suddenly
    night was lit   by a sheeted flame
It fell from heaven   shot through earth's fault
        geyser   waterfall
              solemn   spontaneous
a suspended curtain   a scrim between worlds

Here was temperate air   there   souls steeped in fire
    I saw them hand in hand   a fair company
praising God   in the eye of his fierce purgation
    knots of self love   exploding in fusillades
           flesh extraneous
        or what passed for flesh
           fallen away

They were careful to stand in the fire's circumference
      intent on the dance   feet
    scarcely touching the bed of coals
hands   hands of bride and groom   of friend and friend
           joined in that furnace
        The days of flesh blew away

the days of flesh like grass—
love counter to marriage vows
ungovernable love
love intent on self love
love of creatures   mocking the creator

all burned away   seared   scored in fire

Yet the ordeal seemed pure delight

    Like pilgrims who reach in mid desert
        a sparse oasis
        and linger there
while the world like a mad brand   burns itself out
        they sang like singing birds
           like birds in a nectar tree

Of all things   my shadow most intrigued them

        Impersonal   godlike
          the sun
      stands above Jerusalem
    like a savior's glance   looks down
      on Bombay   that human lazar house
      on New York's towers and hovels
      on Tehran   rose red with blood
        An angel cried
    Blessed the pure of heart!

And I must walk that fire
Must. Walk. In that fire
souls walk and talk
and praise God   a comely sight
unseen on earth   I have seen
bodies like walking torches   under the mad

fire bombers   Now I
risk that fate   by command
of God the fiery   desert God   sun God
God of the fire ball
that fell like God's down fall on
Hiroshima   Must walk—

But what is heart made of but flesh?
Flesh darkens in that cauldron
Heart blackens
like death's eyesore   I must walk—
Draw back   I have seen
burnt bodies   meat on a red rack
those war years   the young hand
like a claw of Lazarus   miming   beckoning death

That fire
that fire storm   How many drank
and died!   *Beati mundo corde*
the angel intones
unverified   until I walk
God's hand heaps coals of fire
like ripe fruit before a child's
concupiscent eye   It is written
I must eat or die   but my mind
appalled amends   *Eat and die!*

O then
lip-read the words of fire
flesh   bones must bear
as fish their element   or birds
mild morning air—

What God is made of
he makes of us

Dante Departs

Sunrise   new world newly blessed
Fire of purgation   hell fire   all endured
all past
I breathed deep as the newborn   dawn
entered me like a wine

Abruptly
my friend turned to me—
So far we've come   consummation
is all but yours.
And I *Thus far is far indeed*
Like feverish sleepwalkers we trudged
hell's grotesque horrors
the smitten freak show of creation—
Then purgatory
its ice and fire   and slowly cleansing fog—

And I must say farewell.

I;   *Loss dims my eyes*
Helpless once
rendered less helpless by your love
Take my heart dear friend
let it be lost in yours
as yours in God's.

And he: *The past is done   the future*
is in no hands of ours
See   Someone walks ahead.

Whose face?

I see no face   But you will see

I remember once presiding, along with an Indian holy man, at a retreat for college students. My friend neither hedged nor entered into silly byways, nor suffered loose talk. He was not present to "dialogue" with neophytes. Take it or leave it was the tone; he was there to convey, embody a tradition.

He won them, the children of technique, facts, figures; that Western configuration of mind, competent, skillful, steeped in self-confidence. He reduced them to silence, he set them pondering. They had seldom been silent before a mentor; they had not been taught to ponder, only to "assimilate," give back, produce. He was dangerous, as holiness should be; he was a sword of wisdom.

I bring this up because it illustrates the method of the school of the mountain. Dante is chastened, teachable; he brings fifty years of life to the wisdom of the dead. We have a sense that he is not pushing his ego up a steeply inclined plane; nor that he knows a great deal (though one would judge that he knows much, is sharp and observant). But his knowledge comes through in reticence; he is a listener, he evokes their secrets from the dead. And this, I take it, is already wisdom of high order.

It is strange, on reflection, that images of fire so dominate the official teaching on purgatory to the point where "purgation by fire" quite absorbs the matter. The content of the teaching seems thus to imitate and illustrate the thing taught, a circle that to some might appear somewhat vicious.

Dante is more restrained. On the mountain he limits the imagery of fire to merely one terrace, one sin. And he places the fiery circle nearest the place of refreshment, the earthly paradise. Thus those who suffer torment by fire are placed in a certain perspective. They know they have all but conquered, relief lies just ahead and, after that, beatitude, the vision of God.

There are, according to Dante, actual disorders of the flesh for which one is accountable. This first of all. And it seems to me a quite special mark of integrity that Dante openly accuses himself of such sins, refuses to eliminate the sin, in order to justify cultural humbug or to save face.

I mention the phenomenon because it has merit in itself; and because dodging the facts of sin has wider implications than the sexual. Implications as wide as the world, as dangerous as time's outcome.

In our youth, for example, that department of federal government appointed to make war said so; it was known as the Department of War, and the functionary in charge was Secretary of War.

Today all this is wonderfully changed. When citizens like us stand at the Pentagon to resist nuclear blasphemy, all but the hardiest are slightly embarrassed to discover that we are objecting to something as virtuous as the "Department of Defense," which now of course has *its* Secretary. Object? to "Defense"? Surely it is we who are flaky in the mind. The sin of warmaking, war preparation, weapons research, international arms trade— all this has been eliminated; we are stalking a ghost. We are offensive to defense.

As things grow worse, language must cover up, a smile on a corpse. And when things stand just short of holocaust, the language must be upbeat, hip. Or it must come on as seductive, sickroom talk. Or it brazens things out, a barefaced lie (as in "Department of Defense"). Above all, every objectionable trace of (so-called) "sin" must be removed.

Pentagonese thus suggests a wide-eyed, right-on insolence, a crafty puzzlement: "We are of course quite ready to listen even to the benighted, the trouble maker . . . what after all can the trouble be?"

None of this in Dante. Lust exists, as the prior six terraces indeed exist, occupied by penitents who have sinned against this or that law of love.

But there is a further degree of integrity here. If we honor Dante for truthfulness in the presence of unpalatable truth, we must doubly honor his willingness to stand under the sword of that truth. Or (to change the figure in accord with his own), he enters the fires his truthtelling has kindled. The seventh terrace is a moment i what could be accounted a lengthy general confession, the ı ..rgatorio itself.

"I must walk those fires." He dreads them. Every bone and fiber of his being is as little proof against fire, as dry sticks. On the lower terraces, in expiation of other sins, harsh decrees were invoked; blindness, great burdens, emaciation, exclusion. But none of them, not all their sum, could evoke this terror, paralysis, dread. From none of them does his flesh so recoil. And the recoiling is not a matter of sympathy, compassion for the plight of others, though this too invades his spirit.

Here he speaks of his own fate, dreads it. He is in the grip of irony; he, the living, must suffer in the flesh as he has sinned in the flesh. Others who walk the fire do so as unfleshed souls. But how will the flesh bear what the spirit can scarcely bear? He does not know, he fears mightily.

I have placed on Dante's tongue words about death by fire; in the sixties, in America, the deaths of at least four people occurred in my immediate circle of acquaintance: the deaths among others, of Roger Laporte and Norman Morrison. Their deaths, the death of other Americans, young and old, men and women, I have discussed at greater length elsewhere with the Vietnamese Buddhist monk, Thich Nhat Hanh.* In Vietnam, for a period of many years, such self-immolations were common occurrences, as the fury of our war struck home there. Such are the memories I bring to the terrace of fire. But who of us, living through that terrible decade, is unburdened by such memories?

Social innovators, those who bring about nonviolent change, tend to be sexually conservative. They are experimental, they

* *The Raft Is Not the Shore: Conversations Between Thich Nhat Hanh and Daniel Berrigan.*
Boston: Beacon Press, 1975.

improvise, they imagine or enact (both) profitable human arrangements in widely diverse areas of life. But in one area they tend to draw back, even to be strait-laced: the sexual. And the same strait bounds are usually laid out for their followers.

This is not to state that those we so honor come to such views from the start. Saint or secular leader, the evidence is other. But at least it can be said, as a common experience, that they converted to this view, this discipline; and from that point, their serious work began in the world. (This would be true of males; of women, the evidence is not in. More properly, it is neglected.)

In those we are discussing, the question naturally arises: Converted to what? The question is difficult, but by no means so difficult as commonly assumed. (The assumption being that responsible sexual conduct is so nearly impossible that it could engage no one in fact.) Let us merely note that Dante assumes such responsibility to be not only possible, but human and desirable. He assumes this by way of retrospection and opposition. He presents us first with humans who recall their former conduct, whether regretting or approving it. He recalls also, as grist for repentance, classical images of sexual sobriety, right order. Thus he weaves around us, not a noose of principle, but a generous circle of lives, ways, hopes, relationships, winning examples.

Here as elsewhere his psychology is acute, to the point. We have had cause to note the method before. It is no sterile dialectic; it is tender, generous, classic, in touch. It is of the flesh, but the flesh is laid on bones; and the bones stand upright. Would we know how the great ones have lived in the world? See then. See their struggle, conquest, reward. He offers us a dramatic structure of truth.

12·Of the Vision of Beatrice

I was alone   twice alone
cast out of the turbid world
alive not dead
among the dead   a familiar   nearly a ghost

The labors of the holy mountain done
I walked where a path beckoned
a gloomy wood
threaded by streams
Thickened by sable branches
incursive dark at noon
put out the sun.

No stream of earth could match
the dark clairvoyance of those waters

And across them
a glance   a life line—
Such glory
as makes the dead
cry out in loss and longing
rewarded   transfigured   my poor sight

Stood one
long dead to my   eyes
stood one

whose death broke the coherent world
broke my heart like a clod
broken   tossed   on the box of death
stood one
long dead   dead in my youth
and my youth dead in her loss
Stood there.   joy   tears sprang to my eyes
                  Tears and joy
fought in me   flooded me   mastered me
Wild with hope   shaking from head to foot
The power of lost love!   the mark of the ancient flame!

            a trecento woman
                far from the modern fashion
            she moved all in white
                in a field of colors

            carelessly
                artfully
            she gathered such flowers
                as light is made of

            Who she was
                how she came there
        waited on my heart   that had braved
                hell's black mood   now
                stock still
                    between beats
            paused   as she paused

            And looked up—
                recognition
            redeemed the blank eons!

Then I saw trees like men walking

They neared   neither trees nor men
but light only   light upborne
and the bees' columns   food of light
upborne by hands   and faces
as though carven   behind the tall candles
Such majesty made majestic words
redundant. Yet a choir spoke like thunder
Hosanna and   *Benedictus qui venit*

A dawn   unlike all others
remains with me
The idle East stood lucent as an eye
but where sun rose   mists like a mercy
veiled the intolerable splendor
A long time I stood   a sun gazer
unharmed

Benedictus!
blessed indeed
A procession of lights   a feast of lights and flowers
and she its eucharist   its heart

Her eyes were stern   her beauty blazed
Look long at me   indeed I am Beatrice
Dare you enter his holy mountain
Where perilous   true joys are won?

More merciful than she   the choir
In you O Lord I hope
let me not be shamed.

My glance fell to the pure stream
but there   my own image
recoiled

an image her stern pity
pitilessly traced

She spoke
The cloud of spirits
trembled
Such promise he held!
You vigilant ones   who watch
night and day before God's throne
to whom no thought is secret—
This man loved me   my love revealed
a good way

I died
his course grew obscure and ridden
The truth is known
to God and ourselves   Lust   anger
were his hallmarks
So eager   so intractable   he seemed
dark counter of the one I loved

How reverse his folly?
he must see the damned
whose fate he courted
must walk those fires
take to the bone   the thrust of God's anger

For his sake
I stand in the threshold   where the holy dead
winnow their grain from chaff and tares

She turned to me abruptly—*Say it*
Do I speak rightly?

Nothing   I could say nothing
She paused   then more gently
Come   speak to me.

Indeed what could I say?
my life lay prone   a corpse
in that place of the dead
and a dead woman   dearest to me
of the universe
judged me

What was it   tell me   she probed
darkened our fair beginnings?

When you were lost to me   I cried
*"Ours" was a lost word
my life   my gain   my pleasure—
the nest of snakes   uncoiled
fed on the day
What mortal thing of all the world
repaid
loss of your face? The demons claimed me.*

The wheel turns back, she said softly
*You thought me dead   you see me living
you turned from living love to feed on shadows
How could it be—*
Her passion quickened
*You grew forgetful of my face
as though the worms should batten on our love?*

Listen. She breathed deep
*This the word of the Lord
Lord of the mountain, Lord of fires and fog
Lord of stone burden   sewn eyelids*

of arrows   inaccessible heights—
Let the priests mouth lies   deception be their rote
let the beast slouch forward
let the house of idols be called house of the Lord
the house of the Lord be infested with idols
let war follow war   war follow peace
let the mighty crush
the recourseless poor
and the stupefied cry out
for circuses and bread
and Caesar beget in his image
succubus   incubus   ad infinitum

> Silence followed   as though
> the mountain breathed deep
> in horror or relief   or both

O bearded man   she mocked me then
Lift up that beard of manhood
Have you heard grief enough? I give you joy.

I raised my sorry head
There
　　　a figure all in white
like a column the bees build
like a priest vested for sacrifice
whose eyes bear the grief
of the last hour

> There Beatrice knelt

Age after age, much has been made of Beatrice. Veil upon
veil laid over this mysterious one.

We had best begin by summoning the meager facts. As a

young girl, Beatrice passed before Dante's gaze once or twice. Later, they met at a ball where, we are told, she mocked him for reasons unknown. And that was all; she died young, he married. His love was lost, of love's labors there were scarcely any.

And he never forgot her. The layering of memory began in him, a healing and fruitful process, a pentimento indeed.

But he was not one to linger about a withering grave. Around the image of lost love gathered the accretions of manhood; political experience, marriage, children, trials of faith, long pondering about "the world, the way it goes"; then blow upon blow, setbacks, silencings; he would live and die in exile.

And central to everything, a point of sanity and coherence, the woman who would not die. She stood there, she created a center, an axis in a dismembered and chaotic world. She lent a reason to things, the power of a life that had once touched his own, acid on metal. More; her gaze rested on his conduct, dislocations, fevers and chills, the anger and pride and lust he yielded to, the discipline he refused.

It was his faith that taught him; Beatrice lived in God. Faith transfigured his dead love, until she came to stand for the church itself, living, feminine, generative.

So he came to see her. The point is, surely, that it is Dante who so saw her; she no longer had earthly existence outside his mind. In seeing her, he was seeing himself, with a clarity we can only marvel at. In the *Purgatorio*, he indeed gives himself away; sinner and reconciled, drawn forward by a love he could neither deserve not quite be quit of.

Layer on layer, luminous truth on truth, the image of Beatrice grew. This was no mere poetic process; it was something closer to ecstasy. Finally, on the mountain's crown, Beatrice appears, loved, restored. She has become his sacrament of salvation, maiden and mother of his spirit, judge and intercessor. Had she died? Rather, she had undergone the cycle of Christ, through death to immortality. As he imagines her, she stands before Christ, the feminine side of God, the cherishing other, guarding, warning, nourishing. So she confronted Dante, his very eucharist.

Such prelude might perhaps prepare us for the stupendous shock of the meeting on the mountain. It is a scene quite beyond bearing. The lover is also the accuser; she comes as a precursor of Christ the judge. What an upset to romantic, or indeed classic, expectation!

We were prepared to weep, empathize, find our "feelings" canonized once more. Nothing of the kind. We stand, in fact, in the uneasy shoes of the pilgrim. Very little of life today (except, say, a sane liturgical sense, or a skeptical long way round the psychological swamp, or a hunch that public violence bets heavily on our cowardice) prepares us for the steely gaze of the dead. Who, as we grow in understanding, appear far more alive than we!

Dante is stricken to heart's core at sight of her. Everything is passionately realized; his love stands before him, the endless toilsome climb has been worth it all, and more.

But the love that meets his gaze is by no means in tune with his. Beatrice is furiously, insistently out of phase; she rushes to the fray, she creates confict at the heart of love. She insists on an impolitic, badly timed accounting, prior to any question of reconciliation.

It is Dante's truth. In our shock and dismay we almost forget it. The scene is so powerfully and immediately rendered we would like to praise (or blame) Beatrice for this otherworldly incursion. Talk about the existential, talk about the bad manners of the dead, the rights of the living! This woman calls the entire scheme of mortal life into question, the labors, self-denial, the ascent of the mountain. She pushes Dante to the wall, implies that his great project is questionable from the start.

All this is passing strange. Dante, after all, has survived the pits and heights, he has come through hell and purgation. Is he not entitled now to courtesy, a courtesy he so often received from the dead, in the course of his climb? But from her—no welcome, only a torrent of accusation, reproach!

She spells things out. Dante is entitled to nothing. Know it or not, he is no longer on earth, on grounds of earthly logic. He stands on another realm than earthly titles and credentials. The descent into hell, the ascent of the seven-story mountain, these are no credentials at all. They are nothing more than a jettisoning of worldly baggage, ego, self-importance, repute, merit. Perhaps he is fit for a further lesson: That now he must wait on God.

Worthy? Perhaps by a gracious gift (whose name is Beatrice), he might go further. But not by himself; not by the iron law of the mountain. Yet he persists in thinking, indeed his life prepares him to think: I have come so far, I have lost so much, surely I am worthy of the promise; of all the living I have braved hell and crawled the penitential mountain. What could God refuse me now, and on what ground?

Surely it is not easy to say, when you are hardpressed, when you have all but died and stood again—to say: All this is not yet enough. To say: Much is yet wanting to me. To admit: When you have done all required of you, you are a profitless servant.

It is Dante who writes all this; he summons his life in judgment. What strength it takes, what astonishing moral sense, to make one's way up this all but topless Himalaya of the spirit. Then on the peak to pause, to undergo a further critique, less merciful than all the others. Not yet beatitude, yet another purification.

The scene is surely a high point of genius. Dante gazes on Beatrice for the first time since her death so many years before. He turns our attention, fascinated, astonished, on her. And she comes off best, as he is humiliated.

Among many marvelous aspects of the scene, one is most striking. Beatrice judges Dante. In raising her to the estate of accuser, Dante is in effect undertaking a fierce critique of his culture. Through Beatrice, he breaks the mold of courtly love: woman as unattainable, adorable, object, emblem, victim. Through Beatrice, he calls a halt to errant cultural frippery.

Around this woman there hovers a nimbus; but it is hardly the light around a conventional saint. She greets him with a transcendent défi, a cry of anger. She challenges his male understanding, whether of her or of himself. She challenges his achievement, the conquest of hell and purgatory. Under those eyes, in that scorching presence, human and glorious at once, his frame turns to water.

Undeniably, Beatrice stands surrogate for a higher order of justice. But there is more; something personal, an anger close to the bone. Betrayal, an agreement torn up. He had known her on earth, pursued their love; years later he won her, won over death itself. But betrayal intervened. The accusation is the confession. He had entered a covenant, had pronounced vows to the great dead. And so had she, as she insists, in "rising from the flesh to the spirit."

Sin is betrayal. The "fifty-year-old public man" looks back; his heart is filled with dismay. It is enough to stop one's blood in its tracks. We are not used to such scenes, we are not used to such Christianity. We go through the motions of vice and virtue; we live grudgingly and die in cold beds. The world is not greatly worse or better for our passing, which in any case is a ghostly blur, hardly troubling to the great powers, whether of evil or good, the immense drama of salvation. And that, as they say in the necropolis, is all.

Hardly. Are we tempted to forget, time and again, in the intensity of the encounter with Beatrice, that the meeting never took place? Perhaps, for esthetic reasons, we would prefer to forget. The act of creation, the persuasive genius of Dante, all tend to enchantment. We are stunned, lulled perhaps, by the perfection of this art.

But Dante has something more in mind: the journey of his soul. Beatrice is that better part of him, that possibility made perfect, the eternally agitated, the perfection that will not rest, the image of the God who will not finally be silenced. "Tell the truth!" she cries. "Not enough my accusing truth; tell it with your whole soul!"

13·The Earthly Paradise

Christ and the Church

About that center   a scene unfolded
like a living rose—
true adorers and believers
former hucksters   highwaymen and whores
Priests who bore the single mind
the fervent eye of discipleship
and clerics like pears and pigs   once rutting and rotting
and parents devout   children milling like colts
and captains of the world   uneasy and creaking in their
     straitjackets   (loosed now   that suffocating power)
and factions and fictions   first world   second world   third
world
     they marched into the circle   their banners
     many tongued
Si Vis Pacem, Prepara Bellum!
     The slogans crossed out; the banners read simply: *Dona
     Nobis Pacem.*
Then in silk suits, discreet brief cases, bankers and
     dollar dealers   their abstracted look   like engraved faces
and artists   mountebanks   musicians   jugglers   mimes
and word charmers   and gurus false and true
then multitudes of nobodies   like schools of fish   shaped

like one great shimmering ichthys   like multitudes of
migrating birds
    in shape of one   great sky darkening bird
    gentle   all but faceless folk   their eyes spoke for
them   their
    artless adoration   "Lord   how good to be here"
Then a pride of popes   Popes good and
    indifferent   a weary millennial look bowed
    under the weight of mystery apprehended   mystery
betrayed
And here and there   like lamplighters in a dead city   souls
to whom
    one could entrust his soul   intent on the One
    who above all others   was found faithful
Then tycoons   red of face   congested of throat   like sacks of
money
    tied and tagged
They came   hand in hand with the poor   who spoke for them
    sponsored them—
Is this enough?
That vast pushy dusty hungry unchurched
    fervent throng
hoping against hope   believing and faithless (once)   selling
out and
    buying in (formerly)   chin up and hang dog
And after all (the time is close to after all)   this in their
favor—
they are not formless   drifters spinning with shift of tide
    or wind
but a vast yeasty ferment
yes   an epicenter   true point and eye   simplicity itself
The weird overhead process of fish and bull   virgin and scales
neither defines nor deflects them
Purpose!
hints   invitations   inklings

They shift from foot to foot   bear heat and thirst
a very mix and muddle of creation   recognizable to anyone
who is part of it   longs to be part of it
And then
always those few   comparatively few
who must not be lost sight of   though they have neither skill
        nor will   at commanding attention
for our sake   and theirs   they must not be lost sight of—
The prisoners for justice' sake   the martyrs   the naysayers
the intractable ones
the irreformable   unrehabilitatable ones
those who under every sun   every political flag   every spasm
of crowds
        of jut-jawed bemedaled mobsters
keep a kind of Last Day Cool
an unswipeable smile
a passionate distance
from Blah and Blight and The Next Hard Riding Messiah
        Over the Hill
Let us accord honor   let us make way for these   as they file
        toward the center
where they truly belong
In rags and stripes and newly struck chains
They hardly remind one   of tigers or griffins or heroes
Nonetheless   the throng   makes way for them
dividing itself   in two   like a divided sea
See!   after endless years
sons   sisters   friends
from exile delivered   from gulags   from kangaroo
courts   from torture   from
        unjust sentence   from seizure of fortune
from Devil's Islands   from Siberias   from tiger cages
        from interrogation centers   from ghettoes   reserves
from colonels and shahs and juntas and sheriffs delivered
from starvation delivered

and above all   beyond all   miracle of all
from death delivered!
See now
in the grey faces
and skinny bones
and silence long as the spool of the fates—
here   the human venture vindicated!
Here   the philosopher's stone and
Lost Atlantis and
Shangri-la and
modest utopia!

They near
The Lord looks up   the multitude folds in   like
      living dough
How long O Lord   how long?   has been their plaint
Now   This moment   His look   somber
      self collected   the look of one who   endures
      comes through (but barely)—
that look breaks the glacial will of God
They embrace   one after another
Tears   laughter   two weathers
      contending in one sky

DATE DUE

FEB 8 1986			
FEB 2 2 1986			
APR 1 4 1986			